GETTING
UNSTUCK

… breaking limits, rising above the status quo
and multiplying your success

Dear Nancy Demoss W.
with the Compliments
of the Author

'SEGUN ADEPOJU

12/29/2021

GETTING UNSTUCK

Unless otherwise noted, Bible quotations are taken from the Holy Bible, King James Version (KJV). Copyright 1982 by Thomas Nelson, Inc., publishers.
Scripture quotations marked:
NIV are from the Holy Bible, New International version.
AMP are from the Holy Bible, Amplified Version.
MSG are from the Holy Bible, The Message.
ASV are from the Holy Bible, American Standard Version.
BSB are from the Holy Bible, Berean Study Bible .
ESV are from the Holy Bible, English Standard Version.
NLT are from the Holy Bible, New Living Translation Version.

Paperback ISBN 13: 978-1-952098-67-3
eBook ISBN 13: 978-1-952098-69-7

Published By Cornerstone Publishing
A Division of Cornerstone Creativity Group LLC
www.thecornerstonepublishers.com

ORDERING INFORMATION:

To order this book, please write to:
gettingunstuckwithmenow@gmail.com
Twitter : SegunAdepoju12
Facebook: Segun Adepoju
YouTube: GettingUnstuck with Segun Adepoju Official Channel

FOREWORD

At every buffet, you are at liberty to select from the menu what you desire and all you can eat. This book, *Getting Unstuck*, is a buffet of critical truths necessary to live a life of success and fulfilment. You have the outstanding opportunity to feast on these truths as much as you desire and make them impact your reality for good.

Getting Unstuck is an exposition on the defeat of Goliath by a young shepherd boy, David, in getting his nation, Israel, "unstuck". When we think of David, we do not immediately think of limitations. Here is a man who achieved great success and made it to the top. He was a great warrior and the greatest of kings. Yet there were many who never saw his potential. As a young man, he neither looked like a warrior nor a king. He was the youngest in his family, and as a boy he did not receive affirmation from the people around him. David's greatest battle in his early years was not against the bear or the lion he slew while protecting his father's sheep; it was overcoming the limitations people placed on him.

In fact, David's father, Jesse, did not think he (David) had king potential. Are you someone who feels the pain of having a parent who does not believe in you? David knew that pain. Worse still, his brothers did not think he had warrior potential. At the time Israel was at war with the Philistines, three of David's brothers were soldiers in the Israeli army. David was left at home to care for his father's flocks. His brothers saw him as nothing more than an errand boy, nevertheless, he was a man with a mission.

To cap it all, King Saul did not think David had champion potential.

When Saul heard that there was someone in the camp who was willing to fight Goliath, he sent for him. He was no doubt expecting a grizzled veteran to face the 9'9" tall Philistine warrior. When Saul met David, lo and behold he was a shepherd boy. Saul was disappointed and he said, "You are not able to go against this Philistine to fight with him: for you are but a youth, and he a man of war from his youth."

Although his father did not see king-potential in him, his "brothers" underestimated his capabilities, and King Saul ruled out his competence as a warrior, David was undeterred. He knew what it takes to get "unstuck". After David finished speaking about his potential, Saul had no choice but to say to this Shepherd boy, "Go, and the LORD be with you." To show you how skeptical Saul was, he even offered him his garment of war which David turned down for instruments of war that he was familiar with.

Immediately you have an answer to your potential, you silence your adversaries. *Getting Unstuck* offers you answers in remarkably simple language. Many are stuck with various yokes of limitation which must be broken for the good and godly goals for their lives to be realized. The one with insight never lacks insightful encounters and delightful victories. Welcome to a journey of insight as you dive into the river of exposition in *Getting Unstuck*.

May your experience deliver victories, success, and triumphs to you and your household in Jesus' name.

Tunde BADRU
Senior Pastor, The Redeemed Christian Church of God,
The King's Palace, Katy, Texas USA.
Chairman, Redeemer's Leadership Institute, North America

DEDICATION

This book is dedicated to:

The almighty God, Jesus Christ the Savior, and the Holy Spirit.

The sweet memory of my beloved late Father, Pa Timothy Adepoju.

My mother, Agnes Adepoju, for your 24/7 prayers for me and your pristine thoughtfulness.

ACKNOWLEDGMENTS

I am indebted to all my family members at home and abroad.

I am grateful for the great team of Cornerstone Publishers, especially the team leader, Pastor Gbenga Showunmi, for the concerted efforts to get this book published in good time.

My profound gratitude goes to Mr. Dave & Mrs. Olivia Owen. I fondly call them Dad & Mom because that's who they are to me. Mom, you assiduously read through every word of the manuscript. You're so amazing!

I am also grateful to Pastor Victor Akinyemi, Desire of Nations, Winnipeg, Manitoba, Canada, and Dr. Joseph Olear in Texas, USA, for their useful suggestions. Pastor 'Femi Babalola, Richmond, Texas, and Pastor (Mrs.) Christy Ogbeide, Hope Kitchen Foundation, Houston, Texas, thanks for constantly being on my neck. You always asked, "How far? When are you going to complete your book?"

My special thanks also go to Pastors Ade & Grace Okonrende, Senior Pastor and Asst. Senior Pastor, RCCG Pavilion of Redemption, Sugar Land, Texas. They have been phenomenally inspiring spiritual parents.

Pastor Tunde Badru, the Senior Pastor, The Redeemed Christian Church of God, The King's Palace, Katy, Texas, I am profoundly grateful to you. You graciously accepted and wrote the Foreword to the book at short notice. Thanks for being a great Father in the Lord that you are. God bless you sir.

To my big brother who also doubles as a mentor to me, Pastor Tony

Odugunwa, the Senior Pastor, The Redeemed Christian Church of God, Mt. Zion Parish, Atlanta, Georgia, and Pastor (Mrs.) Christy Odugunwa (Mummy), I say a big thank you for your counsel, guidance, and support. God bless you abundantly.

I am grateful to numerous people whose names are not mentioned but who immensely supported me in diverse ways.

Finally, and importantly, a million thanks to my wife, Christy and to our lovely children for their special support and inspiration in the course of making this book a reality. You guys rock!

CONTENTS

1

INTRODUCTION

Welcome to the Arena Called Life

—

Where's Your Place?

"Saul and the Israelites assembled and camped in the Valley of Elah and drew up their battle line to meet the Philistines. The Philistines occupied one hill and the Israelites another, with the valley between them."

- I Sam 17:2-3, NIV

"The Character Ethic is based on the fundamental idea that there are principles that govern human effectiveness - natural laws in the human dimension that are just as real, just as unchanging and unarguably "there" as law such as gravity are in the physical dimension."

- Stephen R. Covey

"We shall not fail or falter. We shall not weaken or tire. Neither the sudden shock of battle nor the long-drawn trials of vigilance and exertion will wear us down. Give us the tools and we will finish the job."

- Winston Churchill

"If you will not fight for right when you can easily win without bloodshed; if you will not fight when your victory is sure and not too costly; you may come to the moment when you will have to fight with all the odds against you and only a precarious chance of survival. There may even be a worse case. You may have to fight when there is no hope of victory, because it is better to perish than to live as slaves."

- Winston Churchill

11

THE ARENA OF LIFE'S BATTLES

The *Valley of Elah*, named after its distinctive trees, was a unique location in Israel's history. It was the historic arena where the Israelites and Philistines camped opposite each other, and where David Killed Goliath. Though each side started by maintaining its position, a time came when Israel started retreating in fear, hearing Goliath's murderous threats and curses. But that did not last long. A volunteer fighter, David Jesse, filled with enthusiasm changed the game. All protocols suspended. Relying on the Power of the God of Israel, he confronted and killed Goliath.

We all share similar experiences with the Israelites, even though our *Valley of Elah* might be our minds and other locations where devil keeps contending with our respective purposes. The arena called life, like the Valley of Elah, provides neutral ground where we fight, and keep fighting till we bid life farewell. You are meant to fight the moment you chose to belong to God's camp. Even so is anyone who chooses to be in devil's camp - he must inevitably fight because there is no sweet dream in the jungle.

The agelong battle began when God cursed serpent for deceiving Eve to disobey God's instructions by eating the forbidden fruit. "And I will put enmity (open hostility between you and the woman, And between your seed (offspring) and her Seed; He shall [fatally] bruise your head, And you shall [only] bruise His heel." (Gen 3:15, AMP).

We all find ourselves at different times in the Israelites' situation when we're threatened by our fears, limitations, and inabilities.

Unfortunately, many people, including church leaders, pastors, ministers, vicars, chaplains, bishops, and the likes of King Saul, are fast retreating in fear from their goals and dreams.

That's why you must "Be sober [well balanced and self-disciplined], be alert *and* cautious at all times. That enemy of yours, the devil, prowls around like a roaring lion [fiercely hungry], seeking someone to devour." (I Pet 5:8, AMP). It's therefore important to guard "your heart more than anything else, because the source of your life flows from it." (Proverbs 4:23, GW). The Good News Translation is very direct – "Be careful how you think; your life is shaped by your thoughts." (GNT).

GOD'S DEFINITION OF SUCCESS

Success is measured differently by God. Men measure success by the achievement of their desires, wants and goals. In God's lexicon however, success is the progressive achievement or execution of God's plan or goal for your life per time. God told Joshua, "This Book of the Law shall not depart from your mouth, but you shall meditate in it day and night, that you may observe to do according to all that is written in it. For then you will make your way prosperous, and then you will have good success." (Josh 1:8, NKJV).

The "good success" that God promised Joshua related to God's assignment for Joshua - leading the Israelites to cross over Jordan into the promised land (See Josh 1:2). If this was achieved, then Joshua was successful. All that Joshua would need was in the "Book of the Law." If Joshua obeyed what was written there, he would have good success. The "Book of the Law", using our contemporary language, is like a manufacturing manual, or a guiding policy.

Here's another example: God's plan for the Israelites was to be liberated from the Philistines' cycle of oppression. He found expression in David who made himself available for the job. With a great "yes I can" attitude! He confronted Goliath, and with God's backing, he killed him. That was a success in God's reckoning.

It's in the context of God's plan for your life that your success is measured not by your desires, goals and aspirations which may be outside of God's will for your life. When you come across words such as success, victory, greatness, and similar expressions in this book, they are relative to God's plan for you.

You will succeed in Jesus' name!

DAVID CONVERTED FAILURES TO SUCCESS

David was a man familiar with afflictions. With his private experiences of loneliness, he groomed the man of courage inside of him. With slaying of beasts in the forest, he groomed the warrior inside. With secret pains of rejections from loved ones, he developed the characters of love for God and for humanity, faith in, and intimacy with God.

With bitter experiences of dangers of the dungeons and catastrophe of the caves, he developed the art of solitude, quietness, resilience, and trust in God alone. Rather than bow his head in self-pity, he would burst forth singing encouraging songs and chanting positive confessions, some of the important principles discussed later in this book.

CHALLENGES – CONSTANT REMINDERS OF YOUR HUMANITY

Sometimes our challenges are constant reminders of God's purpose for us and the need to depend on Him for ultimate fulfilment. Our afflictions remind us that we are humans; that we are fallible and that we are nothing apart from God. At some other times, our afflictions might just remind us that the world is waiting on us to come out with solutions.

When we have godly attitude and positive perspectives of our obstacles, we live differently – better and peacefully. Therefore, having a godly perspective is important.

Consider Jacob. While wrestling with (the angel of) God to overcome his weakness and, in the process, he lost his hip joint. (See Genesis 32:22-31).

That experience remained with Jacob all his life. No prayers changed it. No fasting changed it. Couldn't God have answered his prayers any further? Yes, He could! Instead, Jacob got the best of perspectives - he "raised a bethel out of his stony grief". Jacob's broken hips joint lived with him to remind him that he was a man, and that, God was (and is) God.

But eventually, his blessings were greater than his painful experience: God gave him a new name by which the whole nation was named - Israel.

Your challenges might be pointers to what you've been gifted with, to make the world a better place. *It was the pain and frustration observed in a driver by Mary Anderson that moved her to invent car windshield wipers for which she got a patent in 1903.* The driver of the vehicle in which she was a passenger had to stop intermittently to manually wipe off with hands, the snows that had blocked the windshield. Where is your place?

Don Moen is a legendary gospel musician and minister. One of his songs "God will make a way where there seems to be no way" was born out of a heavy heart and a terrible experience. He had lost his young nephew to a tragic accident.

This is what he said, "...as I sat on the plane, wondering what I should say to them, I began to read the book of Isaiah. My eyes went to chapter 43, verse 19, '... I will even make a way in the wilderness, and rivers in the desert.' Instantly, the Lord gave me a song to sing to them." But he could not sing that song at the funeral because the family requested for a different one.

Don Moen continued, "After the funeral, I was sitting with them, holding them in my arms. I cried with them, and through my tears I said, 'The Lord gave me a song for you.' And I began singing "... God will make a way Where there seems to be no way...""

Don continued, "I made a taped copy of the song for Susan...I knew that when all of the people had gone, and everything was said and done, there would be days when she needed to hear that God was working in ways that she couldn't see."

Apostle Paul is a man with abundance of revelations (of the mysteries of God). Lest he became conceited, he was afflicted by the messenger of Satan to buffet him, the experience that made him specifically beseech God three times but to which God replied, "... My power is made manifest in weakness." (II Cor 12:9).

Paul had a different perspective of his obstacles: "for when I am weak then I am strong." (II Cor 12:10). His afflictions were his constant reminders of God's evidence of strength and greatness. Did God abandon him? No! Was he stuck in sickness forever? We don't know, but we know that he finished his race strong. (See II Timothy 4:7-8). That was a success!

> Jesus is the begotten son of God who became the beaten son of man that he might reconcile "beating man" unto the God of the "beaten son".

He was familiar with sorrow, yet he did nothing to deserve the thorns of horror on his head of glory. "Eli, Eli, lama sabachthani?" that is, "My God, My God, why have You forsaken Me? (Matt 27:46, AMP).

God never left him an inch and His experiences did not cancel or stop God's plan for him even when his "…sweat was like drops of blood falling to ground." (Lk 22:44).

Jesus brought something out of his experience; "…he learnt obedience from what he suffered." (See Hebrews 5:8-9). That's why he is able to save completely those who come to him for he lives to continually intercede for them. (Heb 7:25.)

When you hold on tenaciously to a cause that's worthwhile and keep working at it imaginatively, the result is amazing, sometimes bigger than what it's expected. Your experiences are important to your success. They are part of the larger processes that God makes out of your life. What have you come up with?

Spencer Silver, the man who made post-it-note, was working on a different research – developing new adhesives - when he made the discovery. "I got to be known as 'Mr. Persistent,' because I wouldn't give up," Spencer Silver said. He found his unique place in history because he didn't give up in the face of seemingly unsolvable problem. "You see these computers (in movies) that are just festooned with Post-it notes," he says. "The fact that the Post-it notes just exploded as a product is more than I could ever hope for." That's what happens when you persist in your efforts at solving troubles.

Have you heard of Fanny Crosby? If you are a hymn lover then you probably have sung many of her hymns without knowing. She was a prolific poet and an American hymn writer who lived in 19th century. Though she was physically blind, her inner eyes saw more than many people's physical eyes combined. She wrote over eight thousand hymns and gospel songs. Her incredible enthusiasm was legendary. But things did not start quite fine with her.

17

Fanny lost her mother when she was a few weeks old, and her father died when she was about six months old. Then another tragedy struck when she was about six years old – her eyes developed inflammation. The medical procedures in effort to save her eyes went bad. Her optic nerves were damaged, and she became blind. Her maternal grandmother raised her and taught her how to memorize Bible passages.

> God used Fanny Crosby to prove that disability does not exist with God. Though physically blind, Fanny's mental ability was exceptional.

Rather than resign to the fate of a disabled child, she turned her "hurts into halos", if I can use Robert Schuller's words of his book, "Turning Your Hurts Into Halos."

Fanny Crosby was an epitome of most, if not all the principles discussed in this book – godly attitudes, forgiveness, dependence on God, faith, determination, synergy, maturity that comes from experiences, craftmanship, positive confessions and voice commands, songs of testimonies. Like David, her different, positive perspective to life's besetting odds is almost unrivaled.

Though she could not physically see, she developed a positive perspective that characterized her hymns which are as rich as the stories behind them. Her attitude was that she would identify Jesus by the prints of nails in His hands. Hence she wrote, "I shall know him by the prints of nails in his hands."

Fanny was conscious of the chords of her redeeming Father, the Almighty God, and wrote that she was "redeemed, redeemed, redeemed by the blood of the lamb...his child and forever...". She also declared, despite her challenges, "Praise Him, Praise Him, Jesus Our Blessed Redeemer."

The physical world might have taught her of its dithering hope, but she was certain of one thing – "Blessed Assurance, Jesus Is Mine", and having experienced the joy of telling others about Jesus Christ, she wrote, "Rescue the Perishing…"

Your prayers (like Apostle Paul's) are not potent enough to override God's will in your life, neither are your good deeds (like Dorcas' in Acts 9:36) able to change or undermine God's glory in your afflictions. You might even be a useful steward in God's house (like the Centurion in Luke 7:5) whose excellent stewardship nevertheless didn't stop the painful sorrowful experience of the loss of family member.

> Your experiences don't cancel God's purpose at any time. Whatever your experiences are, they are meant to mature you into God's purpose for your life - to get you unstuck. You might have prayed enough, and nothing has happened physically but that doesn't conclude that nothing happens absolutely; God's purpose happens in the long run.

I have defined conflicts to be a state of life when your expectations don't match your experiences. And we are in this state quite often. Sadly, this is where a lot of people cave in and resign to fate or settle for crumbs or take mediocre decisions that ultimately mar their lives because they can't bounce back from the effects of some of those decisions. Without resilience, many people break down irrecoverably in the times of failures, setbacks, or downturn.

There was a man named Joseph who kept a resilient attitude that made him fulfil his purpose. He grew up in Ireland but migrated to Canada as a young lad. He had completed a college degree in Dublin, Ireland and things were going well for him. He was engaged and just a day to his wedding, his fiancée fell into a river and died, while Joseph watched helplessly.

In search of a better life, Joseph travelled to Canada where he became a tutor to some young pupils. There he met a pretty lady by the name of Eliza Roche and fell in love with her. They had planned their wedding in excitement of a blissful life together thereafter but again, tragedy struck. Eliza died of pneumonia before the wedding.

But in all these ordeals, Joseph did not let go of his faith in Christ Jesus. In fact, he had composed a poem that reflected his friendship and bonding with Jesus, which he kept near his bed, and which he later sent to his ailing mother in Ireland. He could not visit her due to some constraints. Joseph believed that his mother would be greatly comforted with the message in it.

That was Joseph M. Scriven, the 18th century poet and missionary. The poem happened to be one of the best encouraging hymns of all time – "*What a Friend We Have in Jesus*"! Its first stanza was written on the monuments built in his honor. The second stanza defines resilience in simple terms:

"Have we trials and temptations?
Is there trouble anywhere?
We should never be discouraged
Take it to the Lord in prayer."

The point I am making here is that when we are never tired of telling God our troubles, we are resilient. When we are not tired of learning new skills to improve ourselves, we are resilient. When we don't lose hope but keep taking the steps of faith each day, we are resilient. When we keep a network of people of great attitudes, synergizing with like-minded people of strength, we are resilient.

> When all fears tell us to back out in fear, to look down in trepidation, and threaten us with death like Goliath, but when we dare our fears and take required actions despite our fears, we are resilient. Yes, we are resilient when we bounce back with enthusiasm and refuse to give up!

YOUR SUCCESS IS POSSIBLE

The best way to proceed in any life's endeavor is to venture with the mentality that your success is possible if you don't give up. The story of builders of the *Tower of Babel* is a good example.

Through the ages, men and women have taken a stand at various points to solve human problems and help humanity. They've made the world better today for our safety and enjoyment. Their interventions range from deliverance from oppression, health care solutions, ease of transportation, to political transformations, and they have changed lives through gospel missions, science, technology, racial and social justice, food and nutrition, primitive cultures abolition, to mention a few.

Deborah, Esther, and Ruth were frontline Bible valiant characters who stood against oppression and injustice from oppressors. Mary Slessor stood against barbaric cultures that believed that twin births was a taboo and one of such was worthy of death. She won this battle in the West African county of Nigeria nearly a century ago.

The Wright Brothers - Wilbur and Orville - dared naysayers who concluded that human beings could not fly above certain altitude and yet remain alive. They did the impossible, flew the first flight in 1903 and solved human and cargo transportation challenges in a significant way.

Abraham Lincoln, "Abbey", the arguably unrivaled man in history when it comes to the high-level political defeats, finally redefined failures and eventually became the 16th President of the United States (1861-1865). I remember the first time I read his biography, *The Prairie Years* when I was in College, I was like, "who's this man with a long history of failures?"

William Tyndale was a unique vessel of God; he allowed himself to be used of God for the translation of the Holy Bible into the English Language. Though brutally persecuted, he became greater in death than in his lifetime. Now, we read the Bible in English Language.

Our contemporary world is equally full of modern inventions that have significantly improved our holistic experience of life and our interaction with our environment.

STUCK IN PRETENSE

Our ignorance or pretense does not dismiss the existence of our respective challenges.

We may be professors, lawyers, doctors, engineers, technologists, accountants, teachers, priests, parishioners, bishops, business executives and the smartest of fellows in our different fields of endeavors. Instead of "playing ostrich" we should unmask our cover of pretense and confront those challenges head-on with God-inspired actions.

We all have our respective giants that we think of, and quake with fear, openly or secretly, expressed or in the deepest recesses of our hearts. Like the house of Israel, we represent the inseverable aggregates of dry bones when we are repressed and chained down by our fears, unrewarding career, bad health, failed business, and toxic relationships.

We might have been faking it, pretending that we are happy, pretending that we are successful and pretending to be on top of the world when we wish night hours never came because of chronic insomnia. Of what use is the mattress when we could not sleep? Of what use is the rich bank account when we have bad health? Of what use is peace at home when we have chaos outside? We are stuck!

We pretend that all is well but soon become reclusive and harvest barren fruits of regrets as we advance in age with our dreams getting much more distant, each passing day. We are stuck!

We may be living in great nations with best political or economic advantages, having the greatest numbers of rich people and successful corporate organizations but we might be dry bones as long as we have all manners of prejudices, injustices and insecurities that plague us internally and externally where we feel cracked, vulnerable at the slightest instance of chaos and negative forces. We are stuck!

So, then what do we do? Where are you standing? Now? Later? Forever? What is your place in history? Are you stuck by cycles of limitations? Stalled by *giant* called failure? Felled by unknown stoppers of destinies that mask themselves with cloak of bad health, addictions, injustices, prejudices, and hostilities? Chained by fear of failure? Entombed by thoughts of limitations?

Don't look too far for answers. But if you already know your place, this book will beam wider searchlight into your routing guidance to destiny. If otherwise, then the **new insights** on David *versus* Goliath will help you redefine your life as you become unstuck.

We are not located at the Valley of Elah. Not anymore.

Welcome to the arena called life!

2

YES, I CAN

Law of Attitude

"David said to Saul, "Let no one lose heart on account of this Philistine; your servant will go and fight him.""

- I Sam 17:32, NIV

"This above all: to thine own self be true, And it must follow, as the night the day, Thou canst not then be false to any man."

- Polonius, in Shakespeare's 'Hamlet'

"Attitude is a little thing that makes a BIG difference."

- Winston Churchill

I was on board Southwest flight from the Hobby International Airport, Houston, recently in the wake of resurgence of Covid-19 pandemic that had killed thousands of people and kept many more hospitalized across the United States. It was a period of palpable fear and social reengineering as many detached themselves from crowded areas including airports for the safety of their health. It was certainly a difficult time for airlines and travel companies as the restriction on physical gatherings and prioritization of virtual meetings for various purposes discouraged people from traveling by air.

As our plane was about touching down at the Dallas Airport, the crew announced that all passengers should prepare for landing.

Then a sonorous voice rented the space in our ears. She converted the usual words of appreciation into a song, appreciating the passengers for choosing Southwest Airlines, requesting further patronage as she wished all of us a happy holiday (which was starting in about three weeks). It was a soprano voice in its pitch of fervor. There was a uniform silence at once. You could see the mien of questions on everyone's face, wondering, *"where's this cool voice coming from?"* And when she was done, there was random clapping that greeted her rendition in exciting approval.

What an attitude! What a customer service! Instantly, I determined to fly Southwest airline next time. The reason was beyond the cool music or the voice. I am used to good music; my wife is a gospel musician and sings *alto*. The reason was because of their attitude. What a way to go in the time of dull global mood and flying apathy!

THE LAW OF ATTITUDE

Simply put, the law of attitude states that ***attitude creates everything, nurses everything or kills everything; attitude therefore is everything***! It encompasses your mindset, approach, demeanor, disposition, and the way you conduct all affairs of life, including prayers to God.

I like the way Stan Toller put it. "Your attitude is the basic lens or frame through which you see yourself, the world, and other people. You can have a positive attitude or negative one, and you'll see the world accordingly."[1]

YOUR ATTITUDE IS A GATEWAY OF BLESSING

Everything you are asking from God is almost always going to pass through another person to get to you. God would not come down physically to hand over your blessings to you. Your attitude therefore should be to build and not to burn bridges. You may think, *"God will force people to deliver what belongs to me"*. That might be true to some extent, but you must realize that the blessings you receive through willing benefactors are more desirable than those received through unwilling people.

There's more to attitude than your behavior, poise or look. It's a spirit that is manifesting in different ways and manners; it predisposes you to receive or lose some benefits. When it's negative, it's a liability. But when it's positive, it's an asset because it confers certain benefits on you.

To get to your destined success, you must keep good and positive attitudes – toward God, to yourself, to the obstacles, and to other people. Let us consider them one after the other.

YOUR ATTITUDE TOWARD GOD

You are God's investments and your attitude toward Him is a reflection of your returns to Him which include gratitude, prayer, love, and obedience. Let's discuss them briefly.

GRATITUDE

Gratitude is from Greek word, *"Eucharistic"* which means "thankfulness". Its Latin equivalent, *"Gratus"*, means "thanks". It is the attitude of being grateful, usually in reference to our relationships with God. It is a gesture of thanks and appreciation, especially in return for act of kindness. God has done more than enough for you that requires a return of your attitude of gratitude.

Gratitude is a way of worshipping God which may come in different forms – praises, songs, adoration and in substance, materially. Psalm 50:23 says, "He who offers a sacrifice of praise *and* thanksgiving honors Me; And to him who orders his way rightly [who follows the way that I show him], I shall show the salvation of God." (AMP). Thus, your attitude of gratitude is a gateway to God's salvation (help).

Your attitude of gratitude therefore transcends your earthly life. When you get to heaven, you'll still continue in it.

Like David, we can then boldly proclaim, "Because the Lord is my Shepherd, I have everything I need!" (Ps 23:1, TLB). Besides, Psalm 34:9 says, "If you belong to the Lord, reverence him; for everyone who does this has everything he needs." (TLB). It is unthinkable to have this type of testimony and not get unstuck!

PRAYER

Prayer is an expression of your relationship with and dependence on God.

Prayer happens when you talk to God, and He responds - it's never a monologue.

> When you pray over an issue, you may get divine directions on when, where, how and what to do to get solutions, or receive a unique inspiration that makes you to see the "problems" in different perspectives. This makes you confident and less agitated. This way, your prayers did not change the "problems" but it changed you. Either way, prayer is a great success attitude.

Any time that Jesus prayed, He either got himself unshackled or got people's problems solved. Hebrews 5:7 talks about Jesus while on earth. He "...pleaded with God, praying with tears and agony of soul to the only one who would save him from premature death. And God heard his prayers because of his strong desire to obey

God at all times." (TLB). For Jesus, praying was a priority. "Early in the morning, while it was still dark, Jesus got up, left [the house], and went out to a secluded place, and was praying there." (Mk 1:35, AMP).

LOVE

Love is the best attitude.

Love cuts across all areas of life. You need to keep a loving attitude toward God and all people. From the scriptural standpoint, your love for God is expressed by your love toward others; and your love for others is a proof of your love for God. Love should be the base of all your dispositions. When you love God, you would please Him and tell others about Him. When you love others with *agape* (open unconditional love), you would be selfless, wish them well and do good things.

Romans 13:8-10 says, "… one debt you can never finish paying is the debt of love that you owe each other … "Never commit adultery; never murder; never steal; never have wrong desires," and every other commandment is summed up in this statement: "Love your neighbor as you love yourself." Love never does anything that is harmful to a neighbor. Therefore, love fulfills Moses' Teachings." (GW). "Love does no wrong to a neighbor [it never hurts anyone]. Therefore [unselfish] love is the fulfillment of the Law." (v 10, AMP).

OBEDIENCE TO GOD'S INSTRUCTIONS

Obedience is a winning attitude. It is a proof of love toward God. As a human being, you are limited in so many ways. It's simply logical and wise to listen to the one who is everywhere, knows all things, and can do all things – the almighty God.

Even Jesus, while on earth, declared, "…I can guarantee this truth: The Son cannot do anything on his own. He can do only what he sees the Father doing. Indeed, the Son does exactly what the Father does. The Father loves the Son and shows him everything he is doing. The Father will show him even greater things to do than these things so that you will be amazed." (Jn 5:19-20, GW).

ATTITUDE TOWARD OTHER PEOPLE

It is important to locate necessary steps in the ladder to your destiny.

One of the several steps in your ladder is relationship building. This is connecting with right and like-minded people and displaying necessary skills to get along well with them. You need this in all areas of your life, including marriage, business, employment, social and religious endeavors.

Paul says, "I am a free man, nobody's slave; but I make myself everybody's slave in order to win as many people as possible." (I Cor 9:19, GNT). When he was with the Jews, Paul lived like them, when he was with the Gentiles (those who are not Jews) he lived like them, and even when he was with the weak, he lived like he was weak – to win them.

Paul continued, "... So I become all things to all people, that I may save some of them by whatever means are possible. All this I do for the gospel's sake, in order to share in its blessings." (I Cor 9:22-23, GNT)

Relationship building is a winning attitude. To be clear, becoming "all things to all people" does not mean that he lost his form or person in the guise of relationship building. Neither does it mean that he was hypocritical. Far from it! It simply projects his flexibility – a skill that makes one blend and get along well with people. There's absolutely no wonder then why he "fought the good fight...finished the race...kept the faith." (II Tim 4:7).

> Apostle Paul's testimony is a good example that teaches that getting along well with others is not an excuse to co-mingle with worldliness. You can have contact with others without contaminations, observe your creed without greed, and win by righteousness.

Let us consider some of the ways in which your attitude toward others can make or mar your quest to unshackle.

HUMILITY

Humility is the fabric of any unit.

Humility comes from the Greek word *"Tapeinoprosyne"*. *"Tapeinos"* means low or humble while *"Phrene"* refers to moderation. When you consider yourself in the light of God's sovereign power, what you get is a lower or moderate estimation of yourself, a lower mindset or lower worth of yourself.

Jesus "emptied himself by taking on the form of a servant, by becoming like other humans, by having a human appearance. He humbled himself by becoming obedient to the point of death, death on a cross." (Phil 2:7-8, GW). The core of humility is selflessness, which is a difficult but important factor in getting unshackled from afflictions.

We often find it difficult to exhibit the virtue of humility because by nature, man is selfish, egoistic, and acquisitive.

Life is pleasant when we share its beauty, love, and blessings.

In Philippians 2:5, Paul admonished, "Your attitude should be the same as that of Christ Jesus..." (NIV). But before he got here, he had encouraged the church in Philippi to be united in Christ. Talking about the virtues of unity in humility, he said, "So then, as Christians, do you have any encouragement? Do you have any comfort from love? Do you have any spiritual relationships? Do you have any sympathy and compassion? Then fill me with joy by having the same attitude and the same love, living in harmony, and keeping one purpose in mind." (Phil 2:1-2, GW).

This is mind blowing. Did you catch that? The evidence of your encouragement, love, spiritual relationships, sympathy, and compassion, is your attitude especially when expressed in unity among likeminded people. The catalyst to express these virtues is humility. That's why he said, "Do nothing from selfishness or empty conceit [through factional motives, or strife], but with [an attitude of] humility [being neither arrogant nor self-righteous], regard others as more important than yourselves." (Phil 2:3, AMP).

Godly attitude freshens relationships, smoothens interactions, and fosters godly unity, all of which you need to move forward successfully in life.

How does humility work to get you unstuck? What you sow is what you reap! Apostle Paul continued, "Do not *merely* look out for your own personal interests, but also for the interests of others. Have this same attitude in yourselves which was in Christ Jesus [look to Him as your example in selfless humility]". (Phil 2:4-5, AMP).

Jesus sowed humility and reaped the rewards - being the bearer of the highest name that commands the greatest respect. (See Philippians 2:9-11).

INTEGRITY

Integrity is another attitude index.

Integrity is character that is trustworthy and moral strength that is reliable. Someone said that reputation is what people think we are; character is who we really are. You have good character when people can rely on you without feeling like they have just left a fowl with wolves, when people can confide in you without having to make you swear to an oath, and when people can relate with you knowing that your "yes" would not turn to "no" overnight. Your level of reliability determines how far you go in life.

Your good character goes beyond your façade; it tells of your mindset, that tiny line of thoughts and ideas that permeate your mind, to the deepest recesses of your heart where all decisions are made. People around you might have related with your façade over time but would not do so forever. A Nigerian adage says, *"a person's character is like smoke, it reveals itself with time."* How true this is when you read about the story of Gehazi, Prophet Elisha's servant!

Gehazi's lack of integrity cost him his health, his career, his relationship with the Prophet, and ultimately, his relationship with God. His greed earned him a curse and he became leprous (II Kgs 5:27). It appeared the Prophet had related with Gehazi's façade for too long or maybe he knew his servant lacked integrity but kept him in the service believing that he would have divine encounter someday. Either way, Gehazi became leprous and lost everything because he lacked integrity.

COURTESY

Courtesy is another great attitude toward others. You must cultivate it.

33

Courtesy is an expression of politeness and good manners toward others, not necessarily because of their achievements, high net worth or prospect of reciprocity, but because people are expressions of God's grace and image.

As in the attitude of humility, an attitude of courtesy is a form of seed that brings back harvests of its kind in the future – good or bad. The playwright and entrepreneur, Wilson Mizner, said, "Be nice to people on your way up because you'll meet them on your way down."

RELATIONSHIP BUILDING

Relationship building is part of the essential little steps that contribute to fulfilment of destiny. Positive, *"yes I can"* attitude is an indispensable step in the ladder to climb to fulfil your destiny.

> Build good relationships with people generally with a sense of purpose. Extend good gestures to others without expecting anything in return. Help others who are in need. Help others to reach their goals and do this with a sense of purpose; you'll realize that the more you help others, the closer you are to your own goal.

Do not get stuck with bitterness; resolve issues as quickly as possible. Develop a large capacity to absorb shocks such as offences and insults even as you develop a large heart to forgive others. The beneficiaries of your forgiveness today may be the ones to pardon your offenses, or of your loved ones, tomorrow.

Things happen in life that we can't control but we can control ourselves. One way to this is self-control; to let go and to free ourselves by filling up the beautiful space of our hearts with love, joy, and goodness of life. This itself is medicine for wellness and good health.

You must be open-handed and freely give to those in need, again, with a sense of purpose, for the beneficiaries of your largesse today might be the important donors to your causes in the future.

You need to be swift to hear but slow to judge, knowing that there is the worst in the best of us and that there is the best in the worst of us. The unevenness of life often brings out different aspects of us at different times, and the beauties of love, relationship, and life soon fade away when we are judged by our low moments. Even-handedness then, is the product of justice, and justice is godliness.

> Develop a consciousness of deliberate learning from every lesson of life and from everyone you are in contact with. Never stop learning. Approach every issue of life with the learning attitude of an astute pupil who wants nothing short of excellence.

ATTITUDE TOWARD THE OBSTACLE

Your attitude toward what you consider an obstacle intersects with the law of perspective discussed in chapter eleven of this book. This reflects your inner lens (mindset). What you do, say, or think about your problems is either out of your ignorance or knowledge. Either way, it's your attitude that determines what you make out of the obstacle.

From II Corinthians 12:6-19 and II Corinthians 4, let's briefly learn from Paul, the attitude we should keep toward our obstacles.

What is the purpose?

Myles Monroe noted that when the purpose of a thing is not known, its abuse is inevitable. The same is true of all afflictions that come our way. A helpful attitude to start with, is the question, *"what is the purpose of all these?"* (See Romans 8:28, TLB).

Paul had a unique problem that defied all possible solutions. "I will say this: because these experiences I had were so tremendous, God was afraid I might be puffed up by them; so I was given a physical condition which has been a thorn in my flesh, a messenger from Satan to hurt and bother me and prick my pride." (v 7, TLB). But when he understood the purpose, the game changed as he received inspiration for what to do next.

II Corinthians 4:16-18 says, "We never give up. Our bodies are gradually dying, but we ourselves are being made stronger each day. These little troubles are getting us ready for an eternal glory that will make all our troubles seem like nothing. Things that are seen don't last forever, but things that are not seen are eternal. That's why we keep our minds on the things that cannot be seen." (CEV).

All things, including your obstacles, work together for your good. Having this mentality is a winning attitude as it gives you a sense of faith, trust, and confidence in God.

The key is to see beyond the problems.

What am I doing?

After you have known the purpose of your afflictions, the next attitude is to pray about them. Paul said, "Three different times I begged God to make me well again." (v 8, TLB).

Jesus also did the same when he said, "Now my soul is troubled, and what shall I say? 'Father, save me from this hour'..." (Jn 12:27, NIV). Besides, "...being in an agony he prayed more earnestly: and his sweat was as it were great drops of blood falling down to the ground." (Lk 22:44).

As Paul and Jesus responded meaningfully and proactively to their obstacles, so must you.

MINIMIZE APPEARANCE OF SEVERITY

Whatever comes out of the prayers, do it even when it does not make your limited sense.

Paul said, "Since I know it is all for Christ's good, I am quite happy about "the thorn," and about insults and hardships, persecutions and difficulties; for when I am weak, then I am strong—the less I have, the more I depend on him. (v 10, TLB).

Under the law of action discussed later in this book, I emphasized the importance of minimizing the size of your afflictions with your inner eyes and start maximizing the greatness of God and His ability to help you to overcome. If you see yourself as less than your obstacles, then the possibility of your victory is remote.

Like King Saul and the Israelites when confronted with Goliath, most of the Israelites' spies sent by Moses to survey Canaan emphasized the gargantuan sizes of the inhabitants and felt too small to conquer them. They became what they said! They died in the wilderness and did not get to the promised land.

Paul determined to magnify God's grace in his afflictions, and the wonderful experience that followed was that he was "…quite happy about "the thorn," and about insults and hardships, persecutions and difficulties…"

Pastor Rick Warren and his wife Kay Warren have freely shared their attitudes toward many obstacles they had faced in life. Kay Warren survived cancer. Thank goodness it was detected at stage one. But even during those agonizing days, she refused to magnify her problems.

Instead, Kay focused on God and chose joy beyond happiness that came from circumstances.

Pastor Rick Warren had said in an interview:

> *"... No matter how good things are in your life, there is always something bad that needs to be worked on. And no matter how bad things are in your life, there is always something good you can thank God for...As a pastor I've been with people when life turns really bad in some tragedy, but even in the tragedy I see some good – some good people coming around to be of help and support to those going through the tragedy."*[2]

Pastor Warren and his wife had a good perspective of their obstacles.

RESILIENCE

Resilience is another winning attitude that you must keep toward your obstacle.

> Resilience is the courage and ability to recover swiftly from setbacks. A remarkable quality of phenomenally successful people is their courage to bounce back after initial setbacks, failures, or downturn.

Paul said. "We often suffer, but we are never crushed. Even when we don't know what to do, we never give up. In times of trouble, God is with us, and when we are knocked down, we get up again. We face death every day because of Jesus. Our bodies show what his death was like, so that his life can also be seen in us. This means that death is working in us, but life is working in you." (II Cor 4:8-12, CEV).

Paul's resilient attitude is further captured this way, "in times of trouble, God is with us, and when we are knocked down, we get up again." (II Cor 4:9, CEV).

Evander Holyfield is a living legend with an exceptional resilient attitude. He was defeated twice in a fight while he was young by a "white boy" called Cecil Collins. He decided to quit, and he told his mother that her notion of "white can't fight" was wrong. His mother told him one of life's most important lessons – if you quit because things don't go your way and you won't reach your goal. So, don't quit!

Holyfield got fired up. According to him, "*I wanted to quit. But Mama said, 'I didn't raise no quitter,'...* "*So I had to go back a third time to finally beat him.*"[3] After encouragements from his mother, he defeated Collins at the third attempt and his ego was boosted.

Many mountain climbers had attempted climbing Everest, the tallest world mountain but only Edmund Hillary and Tenzing Norgay were the first to achieve this feat in 1953. There were many odds against them, but they bounced back and made history. Standing on the top of Everest, Hillary said, "a vague sense of astonishment that I should have been the lucky one to attain the ambition of so many brave and determined climbers."

Luza wrote, quoting Edmund Hillary,

> "... *I asked Tenzing to belay me strongly, and I started cutting a cautious line of steps up the ridge. Peering from side to side and thrusting with my ice axe, I tried to discover a possible cornice, but everything seemed solid and firm. I waved Tenzing up to me. A few more whacks of the ice–ax, a few very weary steps, and we were on the summit of Everest.*"[4]

If you have used Zoom to communicate, then, you've probably have heard of the stories of its founder, Eric Yuan. In 2018, Glassdoor's approval rating put Eric at the top of all CEOs. As of January 2021, his net worth was $15 Billion. But he did not start this way. He was born in China and migrated to the United States in 1997. He was denied US visa multiple times. A resilient man, he had prepared his mind to apply for the US visa twenty times but was said to have been given at the ninth attempt.

> There is no limit to our lives if we go through life with tenacity of weeds, with strength of wildfire, and with the speed of God's directions.

ATTITUDE TOWARD YOURSELF

TRUE TO YOURSELF

In one of Shakespeare's works, is this popular quote, *"This above all: to thine own self be true, and it must follow, as the night the day, Thou canst not then be false to any man."* Forget about the character of Polonius, who made the statement. The truth in this statement is indubitable when you reflect on the value of integrity and its relativity to the successes ahead.

Romans 12:3 says, "For by the grace [of God] given to me I say to everyone of you not to think more highly of himself [and of his importance and ability] than he ought to think; but to think so as to have sound judgment, as God has apportioned to each a degree of faith [and a purpose designed for service]." (AMP). "…I ask you not to think of yourselves more highly than you should. Instead, your thoughts should lead you to use good judgment based on what God has given each of you as believers." (GW).

Success begins at the point when you are true to yourself. And this means, honest, sincere evaluation of your worth; self-consciousness, not valuing yourself beyond measure. When you consider before spending, reflect before speaking, evaluate before borrowing, and think before acting, then you can't fall short of being true to yourself. That's the state when honesty is the best policy.

SELF CONFIDENCE

One day during a Bible study, someone asked me the difference between self-confidence and arrogance. My answer was simple.

Self-confidence is a feeling of trust in your God-given strength, ability, and sense of judgment on certain tasks. For example, when he was beckoned to rescue the Israelites from the Midianites, Gideon felt he could not but "Then the Lord turned to him and said, "Go with the strength you have, and rescue Israel from the Midianites. I am sending you!" (Judges 6:14, NLT). He lacked self-confidence.

Self-confidence is not limited by physical or anatomical imperfections because it is personal enthusiasm that galvanizes you into winning steps. Moses showed a lack of self-confidence by giving his speech defect as an excuse when God sent him to Pharaoh, King of Egypt, to deliver the Israelites. But God corrected him.

> "But Moses said, "No, LORD, don't send me. I have never been a good speaker, and I haven't become one since you began to speak to me. I am a poor speaker, slow and hesitant." The LORD said to him, "Who gives man his mouth? Who makes him deaf or dumb? Who gives him sight or makes him blind? It is I, the LORD. Now, go! I will help you to speak, and I will tell you what to say".
>
> - Exd 4:10-12, GNT.

Arrogance, on the other hand, is an exaggerated worth, overrated ability, or undue self-importance. It is in this context that Romans 12:3 cautions against thinking of yourselves "…more highly than you should" which may mean pride when used negatively. Proverbs 16:18 says, "Pride goeth before destruction, and an haughty spirit before a fall." (KJV).

The winning attitude to keep therefore is self-confidence. You are not a moron but God's masterpiece. There is good stuff in you. Use them productively. Think possibility and never look down on yourself. Jesus says, "so do not fear; you are more valuable than many sparrows." (Matt 10:31, AMP).

I encourage you to let your attitude exude self-confidence in words and in actions.

THINK GOOD AND THINK RIGHT

Let us begin to wrap up our discussion here.

Think good and think right of yourself. You must have a right mindset because that's what precedes a right attitude. Every word in the Bible is an expression of God's good thoughts and plans for you. *If God's thought toward you is good, then, you have no reason to think otherwise.*

I received this short testimonial while writing this book and believe it would encourage you.

> *"A positive and hopeful <u>attitude</u> gets me through each day. I've lived long enough and seen or experienced enough of life's trials to know that a positive outlook can have a big impact on me and keep me from getting stuck in a negative headspace. I strive to bring joy into someone's life and/or perform acts of kindness daily to show God's love through my words and actions."*

David's "yes I can" attitude developed a momentum that never abated until he achieved his destined success.

You can chart a similar course today.

3

KNOW YOUR ENEMY AND MASTER THE FACTS

Understanding the Law of Question

"David, who was talking to the men standing around him, asked, "What's in it for the man who kills that Philistine and gets rid of this ugly blot on Israel's honor? Who does he think he is, anyway, this uncircumcised Philistine, taunting the armies of God-Alive?" They told him what everyone was saying about what the king would do for the man who killed the Philistine.

Eliab, his older brother, heard David fraternizing with the men and lost his temper: "What are you doing here! Why aren't you minding your own business, tending that scrawny flock of sheep? I know what you're up to. You've come down here to see the sights, hoping for a ringside seat at a bloody battle!"

"What is it with you?" replied David. "All I did was ask a question." Ignoring his brother, he turned to someone else, asked the same question, and got the same answer as before. The things David was saying were picked up and reported to Saul. Saul sent for him."

- I Sam 17:26-31, (MSG).

"Ask and keep on asking and it will be given to you; seek and keep on seeking and you will find; knock and keep on knocking and the door will be opened to you. For everyone who keeps on asking receives, and he who keeps on seeking finds, and to him who keeps on knocking, it will be opened. Or what man is there among you who, if his son asks for bread, will [instead] give

43

him a stone? Or if he asks for a fish, will [instead] give him a snake? If you then, evil (sinful by nature) as you are, know how to give good and advantageous gifts to your children, how much more will your Father who is in heaven [perfect as He is] give what is good and advantageous to those who keep on asking Him"

-Matt 7:7-11 (AMP).

"You do not have because you do not ask [it of God]. You ask [God for something] and do not receive it, because you ask with wrong motives [out of selfishness or with an unrighteous agenda], so that [when you get what you want] you may spend it on your [hedonistic] desires."

-James 4:2-3 (AMP).

Prompt proper preparation prevents poor performance!

This statement on proper preparation is true especially if poor health condition is looming. In his book, *"What You Don't Know May be Killing You"*, Dr. Don Colbert shares some incredible revelations on the need to engage in early consultations. According to the author:

"I recently spoke with a woman, age thirty-four, who has colon cancer. A team of surgeons had done their best to remove the growth, yet it was spreading in her body. The woman was rather surprised when I asked, "How often do you have a bowel movement?"

She hesitated, then replied, "Oh, about once or twice a week". Then she asked, "But what does that have to do with anything?" It has everything to do with your health and recovery," I told her. It probably was one of the major reasons why she developed colon cancer in the first place.

Our nation may have the most highly trained surgeons, the finest hospitals and the most sophisticated equipment, yet the average person doesn't have a clue about basic health and nutrition. Millions are dying because of ignorance. In the case of the thirty-four-year-old woman with colon cancer, what she didn't know was killing her."

Dr, Colbert added that it was tragic that we wait until a person is sick or has serious symptoms to use the marvelous diagnostic tools available and stressed that much of the enormous cost involved in operations could be avoided if people would be proactive and follow some simple rules for health.

Consider Dr. Colbert's advice: *"Please don't wait until you have a medical emergency. Start immediately to build a vibrant, healthy body – the younger the better,"[2]*

Unlike David, many of us wait till we get to the arena of our battles and obstacles and then begin to ask belated questions. We make consultations after the symptoms had developed and reached late stages. We consult medical physicians after we are practically unable to go to work; after we are unable to lift hands and limbs, or after we have lost sleep for several weeks.

For David, the right time was the time *before* he began his historic encounter with the giant. He did his research, made wider consultations, and took preliminary actions.

THE LAW OF QUESTION

Succinctly put, the law of question states that *every right question timely asked, takes you closer to the solution or to your journey.*

Whether it is a physical journey or a certain goal, the principle works the same way – it takes you closer to your solution. When you apply the law of question, there is a remarkably high probability that you'd get answers that provide the route to the next possible step or course of actions.

David's right questions landed him before King Saul. (I Samuel 17:31-33).

A Yoruba proverb states, *"the one who asks for routing guidance (from the right quarter), does not miss the route."* How true that is! There is someone, who is somewhere and who has solution or who at least can guide through to solution.

David started his mission with questions to get relevant facts to run with. "What shall be done to the man that killeth this Philistine...?" (I Sam 17 26, KJV).

THE LAW OF QUESTION EXPLAINED

God started the first problem-solving relationship with man, with the principle of *question*. This was after the first and the greatest of human problems (sin) got humanity stuck. Adam and Eve disobeyed God. In efforts to get them unstuck, the first thing that God did was information gathering in the form of a question. God asked Adam, "... *Where art thou?*" (Gen 3:9). Another translation reads, "...Why are you hiding?" (TLB).

To be clear, Adam and Eve were not invisible to their maker, God, who created all things. He knows all things, and nothing is hidden from his sight. (Heb 4:13). He asked Adam where he was, to enunciate a principle of *question* – a key to unlocking revelations that help you in taking winning decisions.

That was some hot cross-examination! Oops! Believe me, pray you never have to stand before the ire of a smart attorney in a cross-examination.

Four heavy questions in quick succession: "Where are you?", Who told you, you were naked?", "Have you eaten fruit from the tree I warned you about?", and "How could you do such a thing?" But at least, God's questions elicited some facts from which He made decisions. See Genesis 3:10-12, TLB.

> Adam, Eve, and the serpent were cursed. That was when our major problem became more spiritual than physical or emotional. The sins had attracted curses and man became stuck!

But good wisdom should guide that, if God made efforts and mastered facts to arrive at a just solution (punishment), then we could apply the same principle of *question* to arrive at solutions to our problems. That's David's wisdom.

GETTING THE FACTS RIGHT

Facts are generally accepted truths about a thing. It includes information that is considered relevant in making decisions. Getting past your obstacles requires mastery of certain facts and information about them. This helps you to thin out unimportant details that create distractions. It also helps you to focus on *what* to do and *how* to surmount your obstacles. When you've properly mastered the facts, you'd know what "weapons" to use and how to use them.

Whether your problem is on finance, marriage, health, project management or career growth, the principle of facts mastery works the same way. Sit down, think, study, reflect, and engage in critical evaluation. Jesus clearly taught this principle while on earth.

Jesus taught that, to build a tower, we should first sit down to calculate the cost and to go into war, we must first sit down to consider the strength of our military. See Luke 14:27-28. The emphasis here is how much of information do you have about your problems? Have you assessed the surrounding circumstances to know where to start?

Even God asked Moses to send spies to survey the promise land. (Numbers 13:1).

God's wisdom is deep! He ensured that every tribe of Israel was represented in this information-gathering process so that they would have relevant information to work with as they advanced toward the promise land.

Even though He had struck a covenant with Abraham, Isaac, and Jacob – the Israelites' forefathers – God knew that it was not enough for the Israelites to be *aware* of those covenants. Neither were mere *inspirations* that came from assurance of those promises sufficient. In essence, God is teaching us that, there must be proactive, practical step of information gathering to work with.

Moses sent them out with these instructions: "Go northward into the hill country of the Negeb, and see what the land is like; see also what the people are like who live there, whether they are strong or weak, many or few; and whether the land is fertile or not; and what cities there are, and whether they are villages or are fortified; whether the land is rich or poor, and whether there are many trees. Don't be afraid, and bring back some samples of the crops you see." (The first of the grapes were being harvested at that time.) So they spied out the land all the way from the wilderness of Zin to Rehob near Hamath. - (Num 13:17-21, TLB).

Did you notice the scope of the spying task? Their assignments included the **land's** fertility and productivity, the **people's** strength, and numerical size, the **cities** and **villages'** fortification level, and other relevant information. Besides, to be convinced of the land's productivity, the spies were required to come back with **crop samples**. They went at the right timing – when the first of the grapes were being harvested.

In your information gathering efforts, you'll get to know opponent's networks and strategies. An effective device in facts-gathering and mastery is the tool of questioning – asking the right questions!

PRACTICE THE HABIT OF ASKING QUESTIONS

The Bible says, "Listen to counsel, receive instructions, and accept correction, that you may be wise in the time to come." (Prov 19:20 (AMP).

Are you facing what biomedical sciences have termed terminal sickness? Consult widely from the right quarters. Are you enmeshed in financial debts and groaning under the pains of near foreclosure and financial bondage? Consult widely from financial experts. Is your marriage or relationship enmeshed in the fog of uncertainty? Seek godly counsel.

David asked questions knowing that, understanding Goliath's perspective of his (Goliath's) self-worth would help him (David) master the nature of strategy and size of weapon to be deployed. David turned to another set of people and asked the same questions. Why? He wanted to have wider consultations and deeper research to master the facts effectively.

I use the word, "habit" deliberately because the principle of question is an ongoing exercise that must be part of you, and as close as your ears. That's why Jesus taught that you should keep on asking. (Matthew 7:7-11).

Classically, it was Apostle Peter's question directed to Jesus that elicited explanations on what Jesus was going to achieve for the believers by His death. "Simon Peter asked him, "Lord, where are you going?". Jesus replied, "where I am going, you cannot follow me now, but you will follow me later." Peter asked, "Lord, why can't I follow you now? I will lay down my life for you." (Jn 13:36-37).

> When you keep asking what no one else is asking, you'll know what no one else knows and this clearly puts you in leadership position.

METHODOLOGY

In research, methodology is the specific procedures or techniques used to identify, select, process, and analyze information about a subject matter.

The law of question comes with methodology of how to achieve success and victory. We see this methodology clearly displayed by David before the historic fight with Goliath. It's three-in-one type – *asking, searching, and making preliminary actions.*

When you ask, you make requests capable of eliciting answers and reactions that guide you to your next destination. By searching, you conduct research and make wider consultations with your findings becoming important tools - information - upon which you make initial move. Knocking implies your preliminary *actions* that you take as a first line of actions.

According to Jesus, everyone who keeps on asking receives, and he who keeps on seeking finds, and to him who keeps on knocking, it will be opened. (Matt 7:8 AMP).

Let us consider these tools in detail.

1. ASKING

To ask is to request for information in form of questioning. David asked relevant questions from the right quarters. He asked for information about the giant and the reward for whoever kills the giant. Similarly, you've got to ask questions about your present problems.

If your present obstacle that is keeping you stuck is terminal disease – Coronavirus (Covid-19), diabetes, cancer, hypertension, leukemia, or heart problem – they share the same metaphor with Goliath (giant).

There is at least someone with correct answers. Ask appropriate questions about whatever you are passing through. If your giant is overweight, addiction or wrong career path, the same principle is applicable – ask and keep asking questions.

- **Ask the right questions**

It is not enough to ask questions; you must ask the right questions to get unstuck. *Right questions are those that are proximate and related to your present obstacles and which answers advance you to success and victory.*

In I Samuel 17:26, David asked "…What will a man get for killing this Philistine and ending his insults to Israel?" he asked them. "Who is this heathen Philistine, anyway, that he is allowed to defy the armies of the living God?". (TLB). His questions related to facts about Goliath and reward. Similarly, you must ask related and direct questions which answers would make solutions jump at you.

As an example, asking questions about some lifestyle adjustment needed to overcome high blood pressure or to avoid risk of heart attack for a person of specific medical history and racial origin or family background as you, may be on the spot and congruent rather than tangential open questions about wellness. *Be specific and detailed in your questions.*

Whether you are asking questions from God (in prayers) or from people, it is important to bear in mind two principles.

The first is asking the right question and the second is asking for good cause which aims at glorifying God. Remember that the law of question says that *every right question timely asked, takes you closer to your journey.* Inversely, every wrong question asked at any time takes you to a wrong decision and a wrong location farther from solution. I'm sure you do not want that.

Furthermore, the purpose of your question must be clearly defined – it should break you free from problems thereby glorifying God. Remember what we talked about under the law of attitude that your character is a seed that yields bigger fruits in return. So, your motive for asking must be as noble as possible because if you ask with bad motive that's what you get in return.

The Bible is very direct on this. "…You do not have because you do not ask [it of God]. You ask [God for something] and do not receive it, because you ask with wrong motives [out of selfishness or with an unrighteous agenda], so that [when you get what you want] you may spend it on your [hedonistic] desires." (Jms 4:2-3, AMP)

- **Ask the right people**

It is important to ask the right question, but it is much more important to ask the right people. Asking questions from the wrong people is like attempting to open the door with the base, and not the head of the key.

It is not everybody that has the right answers even if asked the right questions. The pessimists tend to see the world around them from a negative point of view while the optimists inspire hope. The pessimists answer your well-intended questions from the obtuse angle of impossibility, and with breath of hopelessness.

It's hard if not impossible for naysayers to wish you a good end. Someone says that eighty percent of people don't care about you, and twenty percent are happy that it is you. How true that is when you are surrounded by negative people! The optimists however answer your questions from the angles of hope and possibilities.

> You must therefore ask questions from people who would answer your questions objectively after having weighed all possible alternatives. Even if their answers suggest to not do a thing, it then means that not doing such a thing will take you closer to solutions.

David demonstrated what it is to ask the right people. The different translations of I Samuel 17:26 provide greater illumination regarding the importance of asking questions from the right people.

- David asked: "the men that stood by him," (I Sam 17:26, KJV)

- "David talked to some others standing there to verify the report..." (TLB).

- "David, who was talking to the men standing around him, asked..." (MSG).

- "David asked the men who were near him..." (GNT).

- "David asked some soldiers standing nearby, "What will a man get for killing this Philistine and stopping him from insulting our people? Who does that worthless Philistine think he is? He's making fun of the army of the living God!" (CEV).

The context of I Samuel 17 shows that, when David asked this question, Goliath was already boasting with murderous threats against the Israelites and that for this reason, many Israelites took to their heels. If the civilians took to their heels, then it stands to reason that those left behind would probably be soldiers who were bound to not retreat from battles except their captain directs otherwise.

David asked the right questions from the right set of people – the soldiers. I Samuel 17:27 states, "The soldiers told David what the king would give the man who killed Goliath." (CEV). The answer David got was as direct as the questions asked.

Whether you become vulnerable and get swirled by the myriads of life vicissitudes or get unstuck and advance with the speed of light, the determinant factor is who is answering your questions.

> Many people are far away from their solutions because they are seeking counsel from wrong persons and are surrounded by people who should not be in their lives.

- **Ask at the right time**

In almost all events of our daily life, we experience time being of essence - delivery contracts, wages and salaries, commencement of career and retirement from active service, or even lay-offs or resignation.

There is time for everything under heaven. (Seen Ecclesiastes 3:1).

For most things in life, the difference between success and failure and the difference between being deceased and being alive is time. *Do the right thing with the right people and at the right time. Make hay while the sun shines!*

2. SEARCHING

Remember we are on the methodology of the law of question. We just ended the first one which is *asking*.

The next is *searching* for the most needed information and materials with which you must arm yourself mentally, emotionally, and otherwise for success. To search is to find something by looking or otherwise seeking *carefully, deliberately,* and *thoroughly.*

In I Sam 17: 26, we learnt that David asked questions from the men (probably soldiers) standing nearby. In I Sam 17:30, David walked over to some other people and continued his questions.

The Scripture is silent as to the length of time between the episode of verse 26 and that of verse 30 but it is discernible however that, a lot of activities had taken place in between the two episodes which were enough to discourage David from making further inquiries.

Take notice that David's oldest brother, Eliab, had challenged David for his involvement. I tell you, a discouragement of this nature from a respected family member is weighty and powerful enough to discourage you. You must be discerning with whose voice you give ears to per time especially when the discouragement is coming from a respected good-intentioned family member.

Despite Eliab's discouragement, David was careful and thorough as he continued his research. He was dogged. His penchant for solutions to the national impasse inspired his carefulness and thoughtfulness.

Searching denotes carrying out research and wider consultations. This includes information gathering, interviews, questionnaire, survey and follow ups. You undertake these to elicit information as well as reactions which will form part of reports that will serve as tools for proactive steps. This is what Jesus meant when He said, *"Keep on asking..., keep on searching... keep on knocking..."* (Matthew 7:7). It's an ongoing thing.

In the context of *searching* tool, Prov 20:5 is relevant.

"A person's thoughts are like water in a deep well, but

someone with insight can draw them out." (GNT)

"Knowing what is right is like deep water in the heart; a wise person draws from the well within." (MSG)

"Though good advice lies deep within the heart, a person with understanding will draw it out." (NLT)

"People's thoughts can be like a deep well, but someone with understanding can find the wisdom there." (NCV).

"A plan (motive, wise counsel) in the heart of a man is like water in a deep well, But a man of understanding draws it out." (AMP).

Among other possible meanings, I think this Scripture is saying that it takes a lot of efforts to get worthwhile things done - from conception to completion - and that a proactive mindset, insight, wisdom, and understanding are essential to get stuff done. What is then implicit is that a lot of research and wider consultations are necessary to draw out thoughts and get them converted into worthwhile endeavors.

Books and learning materials are thoughts in print, and wise, careful, and thorough research would bring out the intended wisdom and meanings. This is another way of saying that a significant volume of rigorous research is necessary to get unstuck.

Let's consider some components of *searching*.

- **Research**

To carry out research is to conduct (systematic) investigation into and study of materials and sources to prove facts and make conclusions.

In I Samuel 17:25, some soldiers had had discussions with David on the person and history of Goliath. That's information or some facts. David then went to another set of soldiers to verify what he had heard about Goliath and the reward to anyone who killed him (Goliath). (I Sam 17:26, TLB). This is a form of assessment or evaluation. The fact that he did not stop with just one set of people gives credence to his wider consultation skill.

- **Wider Consultation**

David consulted widely; he didn't take no for an answer. He second-guessed.

Fighting your *Goliath* require some form of strategies, planning and contrivances. Your first line of strategy is to get guidance through prayers to God who may then direct the right people to you or lead you to them.

Remember that as you plan to break free from your obstacles, your obstacles too would not relent from pinning you down. You must therefore develop countermeasures and strategies by anticipating the next line of actions of your identified *giant*.

3. KNOCKING

When we knock, we want more than knocking. You want to enter inside or call the attention of the occupant. Knocking therefore implies your preliminary *steps* that you take in form of first line of actions, in the direction of your goals.

Your quest to get unstuck exposes you to the process of knocking which is embedded in the law of question. Jesus endorses this process as a matter of principle. (See Matthew 7:7).

The *door* may be symbolic of what is hindering your upward mobility, but the law of perspective discussed in chapter eleven helps you to determine whether the door is an obstacle or an opportunity.

The *door* may be an obstacle to those with limited power of focus who get discouraged when sighting any little challenge or may be an opportunity for the valiant who may perceive it as an opportunity to maximize for advancement. You must figure that out!

Nations and entities can get unstuck by the principle of wider consultations

The principles embedded in the law of question work across all spectra of life – individual, sectoral, corporate, organizational, and national. A nation, state and city can get stuck and unstuck like any person, natural or legal. They might have been stuck due to poor decisions of their predecessors or of the incumbent, or because of failures of some private entities and other state actors.

They can however get unstuck using the principle of wider consultations to unravel the nuances of besetting odds.

Right questions increase the probabilities of right answers, and this invariably increases the probabilities of our close ranges to solutions. Remember that the law of question states in part that every relevant question asked timely brings you closer to solutions.

Some developing countries are helplessly struggling in the quagmire of insecurity of lives and properties due to the activities of the criminals. Each time I pondered on the lingering egregious waste of lives and properties in those regions, I never stopped asking questions even as I'm equally astounded to observe security lapses in the presence of security officials.

As I considered the possible solutions vis-a-vis the leadership charades, I came to a surmise that most of the citizenries in those countries have not been asking relevant questions to hold their leaders accountable, and if they'd been, they probably stopped asking due to discouragements that stemmed from suppression of human rights by the political class, especially the suppression of the freedom of speech.

If the national leaders would engage the principle of consultation and ask pertinent questions, then solutions would jump at them. Likewise, the citizens should not stop asking questions from the leaders to hold them accountable on their visions, national values, legal standards, and imaginatively discuss how the impasse could be removed. They should continue to ask questions from all stakeholders on what brought the nation to the doldrums, who they are as a people, what their values were, what the values are turning into, and what was responsible for the current value shift.

If the citizens realize their powers to leverage on the principle of question to hold their leaders accountable and to jumpstart their respective constituent representatives into productive leadership, then, they will know that solutions to their prevalent problems are not far to seek.

START NOW

Let us begin to wrap up our discussions on the law of question here.

I remember in those days while growing up, my older siblings would decorate our rooms with different motivational writings such that when we woke up or went to bed, we saw those inspirational writings and got encouraged. One of those quotations read thus: *procrastination is the thief of time!*

I did not understand the word *"procrastination"* and did not even bother to ask. For me, the quotation was too advanced and that I had better leave it that way. To my little mind, *you can only be a thief with respect to material things.* For such a big word to be a "thief of time" was beyond my understanding.

One day I asked my eldest sister, Theresa, what the quotation meant. Then I got more than I asked – *Time is as priceless as life, and it waits for nobody. Postponing what is meant to be done at a particular time is tantamount to depriving yourself of the benefits that should have come to your life had you acted promptly. Your delay is thus a thief that stole your benefits!*

I believe this short story is relevant to our principle of the law of question, especially when it comes to practicing the law of question at the right time.

You have asked questions and received answers, conducted research, done series of evaluations, and come up with a report. The next is to "knock at the door" by conducting feasibility study and begin preliminary efforts that will jumpstart you into the arena called life. This is part of the process that David went through before he found his way to the presence of King Saul on invitation. (I Samuel 17:32; 39-40).

The next thing is to act now! There's no better time than now!

Like David, we all need to master the facts and circumstances of whatever that is our giant that is blocking our motions toward fulfilling our dreams, and whatever that is standing tall and intimidating us, and scaring us from our path of greatness.

What are you still waiting for?

Start now!

4

LOOK AWAY AND FORGIVE

Practicing the Wisdom of Letting Go

"When Eliab, David's oldest brother, heard him speaking with the men, he burned with anger at him and asked, "Why have you come down here? And with whom did you leave those few sheep in the wilderness? I know how conceited you are and how wicked your heart is; you came down only to watch the battle.""

""Now what have I done?" said David. "Can't I even speak?" He then turned away to someone else and brought up the same matter, and the men answered him as before. What David said was overheard and reported to Saul, and Saul sent for him."

- I Sam 17:28-30, NIV

"Let go. Why do you cling to pain? There is nothing you can do about the wrongs of yesterday. It is not yours to judge. Why hold on to the very thing which keeps you from hope and love?"

- Leo Buscaglia

"We must be willing to let go of the life we've planned, so as to have the life that is waiting for us."

- Joseph Campbell

In her book, *Forgiving What You Can't Forget,* Lysa Terkeurst recounts her pains following her husband's marital unfaithfulness that rocked their marriage. She talked about her getting triggered in bad emotions that came from "raw, unresolved pain" which produced "a venomous string of words" from her mouth at a time.

She said, *"Those who injured you are the last people in the world to whom you want to hand over the controls of your life, so that's where we will start. Unresolved pain triggers unrestrained chaos. Maybe dealing with triggers from unresolved pain is not quite as dramatic in your life as it has unexpectedly played out in mine."*

You must find a way to resolve offenses by all possible means, including prayers, counseling, connecting the dots, and soul-searching. The more pains, chaos, and unhealthy arguments linger, the higher the escalations, chances of offenses, and the more difficult it is to control the bitter emotions.

When you linger in unforgiveness, you lose your power to the offender.

Lysa continues, *"Regardless, if healing hasn't been worked out and forgiveness hasn't been walked out, chaos is what will continue to play out."*[1]

Even if your offender is conscious of your unforgiveness, you are in an unenviable position because you're carrying both his burdens and yours at the same time. But the wisdom of letting go helps you to live without any such burdens. It is up to you to choose to break from the past so you can focus on what's crucial about your future.

In Lysa's words:

"Forgiveness is **both** *a decision* **and** *a process. You make the decision to forgive the facts of what happened. But you must also walk through the process of forgiveness for the impact those facts have had on you. Every trauma has an initial effect and a long-term impact. The initial effect in my situation was the discovery of my husband's affair and the immediate changes that were thrust into our world as a result."*[2]

> The wisdom of letting go is to forgive so you would be forgiven, for in this lies the real joy of living; he has conquered life who has mastered his emotions, emptied the poison of revenge from self, and conquered the root of bitterness.

In revenge lies the risk of retaliation which builds walls, burns the bridges, and turns the society to a jungle where none, including yourself, is safe.

The original Greek word for forgiveness is "aphiemi" which means to forgive debts and sins. Therefore, to have true forgiveness, you must first *cancel or eliminate* the root cause of the wrongdoing in your heart. That is why Jesus teaches us that, to have unhindered access to God in prayers, we must deal with "debts" first. "Forgive us our debts, as we have forgiven our debtors [letting go of both the wrong and the resentment]." (Matt 6:12, AMP).

By reason of your humanity in a social environment, you will no doubt offend and be offended. When you are at the receiving end, choose to forgive. *Contrary to what you must have heard growing up, the choice to forgive demonstrates your strength and not an evidence of weakness*. It shows you have a larger heart to absorb weighty thing and not collapse.

The Bible says, "When Eliab, David's oldest brother, heard him speaking with the men, he burned with anger at him and asked, "Why have you come down here? And with whom did you leave those few sheep in the wilderness? I know how conceited you are and how wicked your heart is; you came down only to watch the battle." (I Samuel 17: 28, NIV).

Was David conceited? Was his heart wicked? Was he there to watch the battle? Eliab certainly wrongfully accused David, and this came with a stigma of a false affidavit: "I know how conceited you are and how wicked your heart is; you came down only to watch the battle." How false!

Having been so wrongfully indicted by his eldest brother, David's next natural line of action should be "putting up a defense" at least to prove his innocence of all the three allegations. To be sure, David would be right to pursue a remedy. But, of what use?

> The word, "offense" comes from the Greek word "Scandalon" which means "stumbling block." It describes a bait that is put on a trap to lure and trick animals to death.

David sensed that a respected person like Eliab could be a potential device – a bait - to get him stuck with failure of purpose and chose to move on.

If David had gotten himself trapped in unforgiveness then he would not have experienced the fulfilment of his much-needed purpose – elimination of Goliath and eventual national deliverance.

I figure the then national dailies would have beamed with headlines: *"David Floored Eliab"*, with rider, *"the Macho boy screwed the eldest over bickering on looming war between Israel and Philistines."* I imagine the whole nation of Israel would have woken up to read about how innocent David was discharged and acquitted in *Re: Eliab v David, held at the Court of Common Sense and Public Opinion.*

No doubt David would have won a personal battle. He would have soaked his brother in national shame and Jesse would have buried his head in embarrassment having regard to the larger national disgrace at hand- *Philistine v Israel*. But David would not have had enough energy and inspiration to pursue his higher calling at that time.

Quite frankly, of what use is David's victory over argument with Eliab if eventually they both end up in servitude to Goliath if the latter had captured the nation? What is the point of the victory within when national slavery is inevitable?

What point would David have scored in winning petty arguments when national shame is imminent? A Yoruba adage says that, *when the homes are disorderly, the larger society becomes the jungle!* How true this is!

David channeled his energy productively in showing a higher level of wisdom which unstuck the whole nation. He did not just walk away from Eliab; He walked away to another soldier in search of a solution.

As Helen Keller said, "One can never consent to creep when one feels an impulse to soar." David refused to bog down and get enmeshed in the quagmire of arguments, bickering, malice and unforgiveness. He simply let go and walked away in search of higher level of human existence - finding solutions to human problems.

Unlike David, many of us would have chosen the path of arguments and unforgiveness. You probably would have "shown Eliab that you are not a weakling and that you "know who you are". You would have simply "given Eliab a piece of your mind." But not David! There is nowhere in the Bible where this issue was repeated to show that David raised the issue again with Eliab. That's a great strength in display.

You must not agitate your mind with mundane things so you can focus on what really matters regarding your dreams in life.

> David wouldn't have probably had enough strength to make necessary inquiries that jolted him to fight Goliath if he had dissipated his energies on fruitless argument with Eliab.

He wouldn't have attempted, let alone kill Goliath, if he occupied himself with pettiness.

I agree with Denis Waitley when he said, "Don't dwell on what went wrong. Instead, focus on what to do next. Spend your energy moving forward together towards an answer."

FORGIVENESS HAS EVERYTHING TO DO WITH YOUR MOVING FORWARD

Forgiveness has everything to do with your moving forward in life and much more to getting unstuck. Unforgiveness is a subtle device of the devil that forms a wedge around your legs. The purpose is to trap you in the mire of bitterness.

Unforgiveness is an excess weight you must shed to freely pursue your purpose. Get rid of it! The Bible says, "...we must get rid of everything that slows us down, especially sin that distracts us. We must run the race that lies ahead of us and never give up. We must focus on Jesus, the source and goal of our faith..." (Heb 12:1-2, GW).

One of the ways Jesus "did it" was forgiveness: "Then said Jesus, Father, forgive them; for they know not what they do..." (Lk 23:34, KJV). What wisdom that got the mankind unstuck!

When you forgive others, you clear the path for your blessings to come. I believe Tyler Perry can resonate with that experience of a turn around that comes from forgiveness. You're probably aware of his story about his forgiveness of the man whom he looked up to as father figure. Growing up, besides the pain of negative experiences of abuses from the man, he also had to struggle with whether the man was his biological father.

In an interview with Jesse Cagle, Tyler Perry said, "I don't think it's any coincidence that the day I forgave him, two weeks later, the show began to have success."

When you are stuck in mudslinging or in the turf of unforgiveness, you instantly become lame and unable to move forward. Someone said that unforgiveness is like burning down the bridge that you also need to pass through. Unforgiveness thus has no foresight!

THE WISDOM OF LETTING GO

Forgiveness is one of the rarest concepts that has everything to do with your past and your future at the same time. Incidentally, your corresponding actions also have everything to do with your past and future. For example, if you choose to forgive your offender and let go, it breaks you free from the ugly past as you're no longer defined by and tied to it anymore. At the same time, it frees you to look straight ahead into your future since you are no longer bound by your past.

In Hebrews 12:1-2, the Bible counsels us to throw off everything that hinders and the sin that so easily entangles. I believe that one of the sins that easily entangle us is unforgiveness. It's so easy to keep grudges and seek vengeance which means that it's hard to let go because human beings are vindictive by nature. That's why you are to run your race with perseverance.

To help you run with perseverance, it's important to fix your eyes on Jesus Christ. In other words, get the routing guidance from Jesus words and you would be able to let go as you should. This is when you emulate Him, including His forgiving gestures. Remember Jesus prayed that God should forgive His tormentors. (Lk 23:34).

One of the miracles of the principle of letting go is that it sets free from imaginary bondages because nothing is worse than mental bondages. Unforgiveness puts you in mental bondage as it not only drains your energy but also makes you unproductive.

It's even worse when the person you are begrudging is completely oblivious of your state of mind. He's probably cruising on with life and there you are, chasing the air with fast-wielding fists! There's no wisdom in that.

David displayed superior wisdom, forgave Eliab, broke free from ugly past, and pursued his goal with determination from a heart devoid of weight of hatred. And he reached his goal. He killed Goliath.

He was unstuck because he let go.

UNFORGIVENESS SUCKS

Jesus said, "But if you do not forgive people their offenses, your Father will not forgive your offenses." (Matt 6:16, ISV). This explains why many, if not all of all, get stuck and struggle due to unanswered prayers.

We do every other thing right except refusing to let go of resentment, and we expect things to go well with us. It does not work with God this way. We can't but expect sharp contrast in our experiences and expectations. God cannot disrespect His words. The wise choice is to forgive and let go, in our own interest.

> What lies ahead to make you get to the place of fulfilment of your purpose requires your thoroughness and wholeheartedness which can only be accomplished with a clear mind.

This includes prayers, wholeness of character, mutual interdependence, and synergy, to mention a few. In Peter's words, "The end of everything is near. Therefore, practice self-control, and keep your minds clear so that you can pray." (I Pet 4:7, GW).

One of the ways to be "clear-minded" is to "release" those who offend you by forgiving them. In Jesus liturgical pattern of prayers handed down to the Apostles in Luke 11:4, He taught the importance of forgiveness to get unstuck. He said, "And forgive us our sins, for we ourselves also forgive everyone in debt to us." (Lk 11:4, HCSB). This means that our debts (offenses) would remain on our necks if we let the offenses of others sit on our necks. This is a sure way to get permanently stuck!

BREAKFAST WITH A BETRAYER

After his resurrection, Jesus met with some of his disciples, including Peter who had betrayed him three times during his critical hours of agony. Now Jesus appeared to them too at their critical time when they had labored but caught no fish. That was a good time to *"show Peter that it was a bad idea to betray a powerful man who has just conquered death."*

But not Jesus! He did not raise betrayal issue but instead, demonstrated a gesture of love, even though they did not recognize him. "...Good morning! Did you catch anything for breakfast?" They answered, "No." (Jn 21:5, MSG).

Jesus ate breakfast with his betrayer, Peter. Even though He had forgiven him, Jesus saw beyond Peter's mistakes; He needed two more things from Peter.

First, He had to help Peter to get unstuck so that Peter could break from his past and possible clutch of doubts, guilt and insecurity which must have beclouded his mind, having regard to his betrayal episodes. Jesus communicated with them in a language that killed all doubts – miracles! And so, it happened. "...When Simon Peter heard that it was the Lord, he put on his tunic (for he had stripped for work), jumped into the water, and headed to shore." (Jn 21:7, NLT).

Peter must have reasoned, "...*ahh, this perhaps is the last opportunity to right my wrongs. I will never doubt this man again let alone betray him. Therefore, let me leap, believing that when he says something it means it exists even if it never existed before...*" He gladly hurried into Jesus waiting hands for rescue.

You can do the same now, you know?

One more thing to do with Peter. After the sumptuous breakfast, Jesus engaged Peter:

> "When they finished eating, Jesus said to Simon Peter, "Simon son of John, do you love me more than these?"
>
> He answered, "Yes, Lord, you know that I love you."
>
> Jesus said, "Feed my lambs."
>
> Again Jesus said, "Simon son of John, do you love me?"
>
> He answered, "Yes, Lord, you know that I love you."
>
> Jesus said, "Take care of my sheep."
>
> A third time he said, "Simon son of John, do you love me?"
>
> Peter was hurt because Jesus asked him the third time, "Do you love me?" Peter said, "Lord, you know everything; you know that I love you!"
>
> He said to him, "Feed my sheep. I tell you the truth, when you were younger, you tied your own belt and went where you wanted. But when you are old, you will put out your hands and someone else will tie you and take you where you don't want to go." (Jesus said this to show how Peter would die to give glory to God.) Then Jesus said to Peter, "Follow me!""

- Jn 21:15-19, NCV

Similar questions, three times! Yes, because the spirit of betrayal must be dealt with. If someone betrayed you three times in few minutes, next time you're making another round of deals with him, won't you tighten lose ends?

Even if Jesus would not say a word about betrayal to Peter, He would like to be sure that Peter got the message. I figure this was on the mind of Jesus. *"If I must make you my first ambassador to the unbelieving world, then, I must by special emphasis ensure that you trust me enough before you assume that sensitive responsibility"*.

THE BETRAYED RUNS TO THE BETRAYER

Jesus was the one who looked for Peter – the betrayed looked out for the betrayer. He openly demonstrated forgiveness to Peter – a principle to get him unstuck. And Peter was unstuck indeed. Jesus made him the General (or Serving) Overseer of the first church.

Have you felt stuck and overcome by your past mistakes – even costly one? Overcome by guilt of sin which makes your future bleak? Overcome by your betrayal of Jesus Christ through your disobedience to him? He'll not let go of you; He's looking for you and would not want you end your life journey stuck.

Make yourself available and He would help you.

REPENTANCE GIVES YOU REST

In Luke 15, one of the series of the *prodigal son's* (or should we say *repentant son's*) final actions that liberated him was his repentance. Verse 17 says he "came to his senses" and the step of repentance followed.

Repentance and forgiveness are like Siamese twins; almost inseparable. When he later got to his father, "The son said to him, 'Father, I have sinned against heaven and against you. I am no longer worthy to be called your son." (Lk 15:20, NIV). His father forgave him. That's when he was freed.

The forgiving father ran toward the lost, recalcitrant but repentant son. The offended ran toward the offender. The elated father rejoiced over the found son. "...But while he was still a long way off, his father saw him and was filled with compassion for him; he ran to his son, threw his arms around him and kissed him." (Lk 15:20, NIV).

> Forgiveness opens arm, welcomes, and receives. Unforgiveness however, clenches fist, folds hands, hangs arms, and then either repels or stands akimbo, unconcerned. The one who lives in unforgiveness does not know the true joy of living because he cannot exude joy and love since he does not have them. Only the forgiving are God's true children.

FORGIVENESS EXCHANGES YOUR COVER FOR BETTER

Genuine repentance from sins truly unshackles from satanic bonds.

Having found and welcomed the lost son, the first thing the father did was to change the son's dress — undress the robe of shame, penury, afflictions, and waywardness. He then exchanged them for garment of honor, ring of dignity and shoe of nobility. Then the party began. This is a royal welcome and the apogee of a state of getting unstuck.

You'll notice that the father gave the repentant son (I am not comfortable calling him the prodigal son) a royal treat. That was deliberate. The father here implies God, your heavenly father, while the repentant son represents you in your change of mind for better. What follows is your royal status.

I Peter 2:9 says "But ye are a chosen generation, a royal priesthood, an holy nation, a peculiar people; that ye should shew forth the praises of him who hath called you out of darkness into his marvelous light." *As you are aware, princes hardly get stuck in town.*

Your repentance from "dead works", "empty ways of life" and bad addictions might be the remaining actions left to break you free from your problems. That's why God said, "...In repentance and rest is your salvation, in quietness and trust is your strength..." (Is 30:15, NIV).

God is waiting to receive you into His royal kingdom.

Forgive now and grow!

5

WHOSE REPORT WOULD YOU BELIEVE?

The Law of Choice

"David said to Saul, "Let no one lose heart on account of this Philistine;
your servant will go and fight him." Saul replied, "You are not able to go out
against this Philistine and fight him; you are only a young man, and he has
been a warrior from his youth."

- *I Sam 17:32-33*

"Attitude is a choice. Happiness is a choice. Optimism is a choice. Kindness
is a choice. Giving is a choice. Respect is a choice. Whatever choice you make
makes you. Choose wisely."

- *Roy T. Bennett*

"It's only after you've stepped outside your comfort zone that you begin to
change, grow, and transform."

- *Roy T. Bennett*

"Every test in our life makes us bitter or better, every problem comes to break
us or make us. The choice is ours whether we become victim or victor."

- *Anonymous*

God, grant me the Serenity
To accept the things I cannot change...
Courage to change the things I can,
And Wisdom to know the difference.

Living one day at a time,
Enjoying one moment at a time,
Accepting hardship as the pathway to peace.
Taking, as He did, this sinful world as it is,
Not as I would have it.
Trusting that He will make all things right
if I surrender to His will.
That I may be reasonably happy in this life,
And supremely happy with Him forever in the next.
Amen.

- Karl Paul Reinhold Niebuhr

Like many of us, Lot was faced with sundry opportunities as well as multiple afflictions. He was an Old Testament Bible character with trajectory of multiple unfortunate incidents that followed his choices, many of which were controllable while a handful were not.

Early in life, his father, Haran, died and he had to live with the rest of the family – grandfather Terah and Abram and Nahor, his uncles. Though he had a choice to live elsewhere, there were probably some odds that made alternative choices appear to be out of his control. (See Genesis 11:27-28).

Abram and Lot were able to manage a family-partnership business to such an enviable thriving status but later ran out of wits to manage the success. "… And quarreling arose between Abram's herders and Lot's…" (Gen 13:5-7, NIV).

I think their problems relate to an ineffective management of change. Separation was inevitable and Lot chose the plains of Jordan, near Sodom, the land of the wicked men. I want to believe that Lot should have engaged the *law of question* and conducted a feasibility study (using our modern-day vocabulary), to make informed choices about his next place of abode.

God spoke to Abram on where to settle down – Mamre at Hebron, in Canaan – with promise of giving the land to his posterity forever. (Genesis 13:12-17). But we don't have a record showing that God told Lot to choose the plains of Jordan.

Abram chose to follow the direction, and God later fulfilled His promise. This is the same Hebron that Caleb inherited several years later. (See Joshua 14:13-15). In a twist of fortune, Sodom and Gomorrah, with other two neighboring towns were defeated and many of its citizens were captured, including Lot and some other families. Abram found and rescued Lot. (See Genesis 14:16).

The men of Sodom and Gomorrah were wicked, and God was ready to destroy them. Lot, his wife and two daughters were recused from Sodom by the men believed to be angels who instructed Lot and family not to look back or stop anywhere in the plain but to flee to the mountains lest they were swept away in the looming destruction.

What did Lot do? Instead of leaving straight to the mountains as instructed, he chose to bargain with his rescuers and requested to go to a nearby small town called Zoar (meaning small) (Genesis 19:17-22). Of course, they gave him permissive will; after all, he requested for it. But at least, thank God he escaped the sulfuric fire that razed Sodom and Gomorrah down to ashes.

If you have been counting, then you would have noticed four instances where Lot made choices and their attendant consequences. Let's review one more.

This time, Lot left Zoar for the mountains (where the visitors had instructed him to go earlier, but now at the wrong time). That probably explained why living in the mountains did not favor him. It seemed that the blessings that were tied to prompt movement to the mountains were no longer there for him. He neither had peace in Zoar (but fear), nor a good life in the mountain because that's where his two daughters got pregnant by him.

THE LAW OF CHOICE

The law of choice states that, *a man's choice defines him, and like a mirror, the quality of his choice reflects the direction of his life and determines his courses.*

Your choice is crucial because you are the master of the affairs of your life by choice. Your choices significantly impact the trajectory of your life.

> Everything answers to choice – thoughts, actions, inactions, words, life, and in some ways, death. That's why you must choose deliberately so that you can live deliberately.

It is logical to note that the moment you choose the beginning of a road, you inevitably choose where it leads.

We can say that the moment David said NO to Saul's unproven armor and chose to fight with Goliath, he chose the end of Goliath.

It's my opinion that when Lot chose to relocate to the mountains much later after he was instructed, he inadvertently chose the place of isolation that would bring shame to his lineage and hostilities against the Israelites, the descendants of his uncle, Abraham.

David's choice to confront his obstacle (Goliath) with strong preparations through questions and consultations sharply contrasts with Lot's choice to move to Sodom, Zoar and the mountains through mere sights and personal will short of God's approval.

> When we make uninformed choices in our quest for success, safety, and victory, we often end up as victims of the unpleasant consequences of those decisions.

Like Lot, many people have been victims of their "plains of Jordan" or their choices of the "mountains" at the wrong time where they get stuck with storms of life and foibles of societies. Because of their choices they end up in loneliness and isolation even in the midst of people. They made choices because of what people *thought*, *felt*, or *said*, and got trapped in macabre pits of disillusionment; they're restrained by agonies and enslaved by fears.

In chapter three, we talked about the law of question - the importance of getting relevant and necessary facts about your problems. We saw how David used this principle to get information about Goliath. This chapter is about using necessary information gathered to make choices. What is implicit in the principles of question, choice, and their aftermath is the change process.

Thus, mastery of the dynamics of change management process is a *sine qua non* skill for productive choices. The consideration of the change process before and after choices is a key requirement of change management as nothing is worse than success gone bad due to poor success management.

MEANT TO CHOOSE

Life is all about choices, from your first conscious moment till the last breath. You make choice daily starting from when you wake up in the morning till bedtime.

Given that choice is a daily human experience, it's no brainer to talk about whether we're going to make choices but what choices we're making and how we're making them. The *what* and the *how* of choices are the primary focus of this chapter.

We become our choices with time, albeit inadvertently. For example, we become addicted to alcohol or drugs when we choose to give ourselves to excesses and are unable to control our appetites. We become criminals because we chose to go against the law. And sometimes we become sick because we chose to be careless about our diet, hygiene, and lifestyle.

Here's a principle that you must memorize: ***You are the master of the affairs of your life until your choice; afterward, you become the servant of the subject of your choice for as long as you refuse to change.***

The good news is that we can choose to change whatever is getting us stuck. We can change our relationships, friends, environment and therefore change the course of our lives to a more productive one that takes us to God's purpose for our lives.

I choose life. I choose love. I choose honor, success, and victory. What about you?

CHOICES, CHALLENGES, AND CHANGES

Your choices, challenges, and the attendant changes have everything to do with your present and future life - life after now and life after death.

Choice - Your choice is your life and vice versa. *So, you must be well-informed and choose deliberately so that you can live deliberately.* Let's pause for a while here because the whole of the chapter talks mainly about choice.

Challenge - *You automatically become your choices and all that comes with them, including the attendant challenges.* I use "challenges" because whether what is contesting with your life, time, or success, is a problem or not is a matter of perspective. So, choosing "challenges" over "problems" is a product of perspective that "your adversity" is there to contest with your life and that, in a contest, the choice is yours to either fight back and win, or give up and lose.

Because we live in an imperfect world, we often make mistakes in our respective choices that give us away to challenges. Then, the question is not whether you'll have "challenge-full" choices but how you manage or overcome the attending challenges.

> Knowing what to do with challenges - whether to live with and accept them as facts of life or fight and eliminate them - is the wisdom of the law of choice.

Change - This is where we get stuck most of the time because change is a repellant to a fixated mind. We often find it difficult to embrace change because not all changes are comfortable or easy.

When changes become necessary, even though painful, you must learn how to manage them till you get to your destination. By your choices, you have the responsibility to mitigate, if not eliminate, the impacts of troubles in your life.

In most cases it's not always the case that we fear and make poor choices but that we fear and make no choices. We're not growing because we're not changing, and we get stuck because we're not growing. Like still waters, we're full of dangerous chemicals, fossils - unhygienic and deadly materials that should not be part of us.

A person who does not change lives in the past; he does not live in the moment because the only constant thing in life is change.

I'm not aware of any change which came without choices, or any meaningful choice without change. To be successful therefore, you must embrace changes.

EXPECT RESISTANCE TO CHANGES

In physical science, inertia refers to a tendency of an object (measured by mass) to resist a change in its current state. The greater the mass of an object, the lower its tendency toward embracing change. Put differently, an object having greater mass would have a greater inertia.

> Resistance is part of motion. The increase in motion (or applied force) translates to an increase in resistance. In other words, every change to speed attracts resistance.

As a driver of an automobile heading toward an important destination, you would not stop the motion because of air or topographic resistance. You'd rather increase the coefficients to overcome the odds. This is also true in your quest to fulfil destiny.

Nehemiah overcame the resistance posed by Samballat and Tobiah (Neh 4:1-6). Moses and Aaron saw the end of Korah, Dathan and Abiram who resisted Moses' leadership instructions for changes (Num 16). Pharisees radically resisted Jesus' mission for change from old way of life to a new and living way through Jesus Christ but they failed.

You do not stop because of resistance against your necessary changes. Knowing that opposition and resistance are parts of necessary experiences for the growth that attracts good success, you do not lose heart when the changes to your dreams face resistance. Draw enthusiasm from God as you brace up.

History is replete with resistance to changes - from personal affairs, corporate matters, to communal, local, national, and global levels.

The locals resisted the change wave pioneered by Mary Slessor who advocated a stop to killings of twins who were believed to be evil omen, over a century ago in the old south-south Calabar and some parts of the modern-day southeast areas of Nigeria. But eventually the change came to stay.

As far back as prehistoric ages up to a few centuries ago, women were relegated to the background, denied basic human rights, and were not allowed to take leadership roles in families and communities let alone national or international roles. Mary Slessor left a better environment in Scotland and chose to be a missionary to Africa. Her choice led to liberation in some indigenous communities by sharing the gospel of Jesus as well as discouraging cultures of killings of twins and women relegation.

The physical and social environments were unfriendly. But Slessor would not relent until these barbaric practices were abolished in the early 1900s.

After centuries of resistance, women began to participate and take leadership roles across many areas of life. Now the old *status quo* has changed. For example, an unprecedented history was made in the winter of 2021 when the World Trade Organization (WTO) announced its first ever African and first ever female Director General (DG) in the person of Dr. Ngozi Okonjo-Iweala, who hails from the South/south area of Nigeria. She was a woman of many "firsts".

In the United States, a new history was recently made on January 20, 2021, when Kamala Harris was sworn in as the first female Vice President of the United States in its two and a half centuries' history.

Harris also doubles as the first *African American* and the first *Asian-American* person to hold the office of the Vice President of the

United States. Do not forget that Harris also blazed the trail in California where she was a district attorney of San Francisco. She was also the first Black female attorney general in California history.

Before Harris became the Vice President, she was a senator. In the words of Dan Morain, *"On January 3, 2017, Vice President Joe Biden administered the oath of office to Kamala Harris as California's forty-fifth senator. The daughter of Shyamala Gopalan and Donald Harris, immigrants from India and Jamaica who came to America in search of higher education and better lives, was the second black woman to serve in the most exclusive club and the first woman of Indian descent."*

The significance of these instances of historical changes is a guide to choice-making to the effect that, every worthwhile choice stands the chance of resistance and that making choices is not enough; you must be prepared to defend your choices in the face of challenges.

DEFEND YOUR CHOICE

I remember a Yoruba proverb that says, *"a hunter who shot at animal must follow up with a tracking chase lest the animal becomes a waste.'* This is true because making choices and not being prepared to defend the outcome soon makes the initial decision a wasted effort.

For you, defending your choice may mean preparing for changes by being flexible to deal with the attendant changes. It may also mean increasing your values by improving yourself with both cognitive and non-cognitive skills or changing your health by changing your diets and having regular exercise or changing the direction of your life to a more meaningful one by changing your social, physical and relationship environments.

Make it your duty to defend your choices with everything you've got.

CHANGE DYNAMICS

Let us briefly consider some change dynamics before we get too deep into other principles of the law of choice.

Have you ever shopped for materials when you must buy another merchandise because you bought a certain good? This is not a case of buying one and getting one free. It's a case of buying a complete set because you chose to buy just one item.

Recently I noticed a kind of disturbing noise from the rear side of my car each time I pressed a brake pedal. The noise got worse with each day on the road. So, I visited a mechanic workshop where I was told that the rotor and the brake pad to the right side of the back wheel were bad and needed to be replaced as soon as possible.

The mechanic added that I had to change the rotors and brake pads to both wheels at the back because the pads were usually sold together. I had no choice but to pay for the replacement of the rotors and the brake pads of the back wheels, even though only one was bad.

Choice and change work the same way. *When you make choice, you inevitably choose change(s) because choice and change are not mutually exclusive. This* **non-exclusivity** *accentuates the importance of a deeper introspection when making choices, especially when the consequential variables portend a serious threat to your purpose in life.*

Instructively, there is no single catch-all formula to overcome the attendant challenges. Under the change dynamics, we shall consider *reflections, prayers,* and *cognitive self-change* before we wrap it up with *change management.* These have been proven to be effective in dealing with attendant challenges that come with choices.

Reflections - In January 2021, I had an opportunity to minister to a select group of Christian youth on the topic "Reflections". We considered in detail, the text of II Corinthians 3:18 which reads, "And **we all**, with **unveiled face**, *continually* **seeing** as in a **mirror** the **glory of the Lord**, are *progressively* being **transformed** into **His image** from [one degree of] glory to [even more] **glory**, which comes from the Lord, [who is] the **Spirit**." (AMP) (Emphasis supplied).

The Living Bible translations read, "But we Christians have no veil over our faces; we can be mirrors that brightly reflect the glory of the Lord. And as the Spirit of the Lord works within us, we become more and more like him." (TLB).

Please permit me to highlight the points covered because I know its very importance to our discussions on change.

The word *reflection* is a polysemic word which means that it can have more than one meaning. It may mean serious thought or consideration on a thing, especially when used in the context of meditation or pondering. It may also connote the throwing back by a body or surface of light, heat, or sound without absorbing, especially when it relates to light reflections.

In the first meaning, meditation (on a thing) certainly leads to a choice – to do or not to do, and the mind, like a metallic coil spring, never remains the same again once stretched. In the second meaning, once light reflection takes place, darkness automatically disappears because a reflection has taken place; a change has occurred.

Seeing God's glory through the *mirror* is a choice that leads to *transformation* (a change experience) from one level of glory to another. What we become is *God's image* which brings glory to God through the *catalyst* of the Holy Spirit.

God's purpose is achieved when our challenges give us an experience of a change that reflects His character (image), thereby giving Him all the glory. I was happy (and still I am) for the positive and encouraging feedbacks I got from the organizers and the participants. Glory to God!

Now, this is where my discussions with the youth intersect with the subject of change dynamics. *Change is a necessity for growth, and no one gets unstuck without growth.*

Beholding God with open faces, as stated in II Corinthians 3:18, connotes our winning choices which include reflections.

A perfect way to start reflection is on the Bible, especially on areas that are getting you stuck. *Happily, all areas of human endeavors are covered in the Bible – financial, relationship/marriage and related matters, career, wisdom, health, risks, faith, children, and parenting, etc.*

The more you ponder on God's promises and instructions, the wiser you get in resolving all manners of problems, and the more faith develops in your heart, to receive the manifestations of God's promises. Besides, meditating on God's words helps you to hate what God hates and like what God likes, and nothing gets a person unstuck like godliness!

Prayers - We have seen numerous examples in the Bible who overcame choice-induced troubles by prayers. That's what Jesus, Paul and a host of the saints did to get unstuck. I Thessalonians 5:17 says, "Pray continually." (NIV).

When you pray meaningfully, you see your challenges differently (like Apostle Paul) and get answers in God's timing (remember that God is our present help in troubles). But one thing is sure, prayers would not leave you the same – it will change you, your perspective, or your challenges.

Cognitive Self-change - Remember that we talked about reflections and prayers as mechanics of change in previous pages. During reflections, we get knowledge and understanding of new things, or of old things with insights. In the place of prayers, God may direct us to do or refrain from doing a thing. Either way, for us, mental redirection has taken place. That's what we are discussing here.

Cognitive self-change is about choice, accountability, management, risk-taking and personal responsibility. The principle of cognitive self-change is a modality that targets practical approaches to problems solving. The essence of this principle is the mental stimulation that redirects your thinking patterns, attitudes, values, and beliefs, thus finding the meanings attached to your life events.

MENTAL REDIRECTION

Cain did not practice cognitive self-change when he realized that his offerings were not accepted by God, and so, he killed Abel. (See Genesis chapter 4).

Amnon's poor choice of friendship (with Jonadab) was as bad as his wrong choice of rape. If he had had a mental redirection then he would have interpreted his proposed actions to mean admixtures of crimes and immorality, which were the surest ways to have a ruined life. (See II Samuel chapter 13).

A mental redirection for Tamar could have started with mind control, self-control, and seeking counsel from a godly person, and then get the consent of another lady for a relationship. In the process, he would have realized that lusting after his half-sister was a want and not a necessity.

In contrast, the so-called *prodigal son* later practiced mind control and cognitive self-change: "When he came to his senses, he said..." (Luke 15:17, NIV).

He had mental redirection and got a different meaning of his state in life - a son of a rich father, and not a vagabond! This realization prepared him for a productive choice. "I will set out and go back to my father and say to him: Father, I have sinned against heaven and against you." (Verse 18).

For the victims of antisocial behaviors and negative attitudes, substance abuse, mental health, dysfunction social skills, a mental redirection is important. And this is where cognitive self-change provides mental redirection to develop a different perspective of their problems. It is super important because having a different perspective is a product of choice of a change of mind.

> When you properly redirect your mind positively in times of anger, frustration, lack, inordinate ambition, and excessive craze, you're most likely going to make right, rational, and positively productive choices.

CHANGE MANAGEMENT

Our world is changing in every aspect as technology and unforeseen incidents such as covid-19 and political instabilities around the world have affected the ways we live. This inevitably makes choices more complex. Embracing and preparing for positive changes therefore become a *must-have* for success and stability, whether our choices are personal or organizational.

The social scientist, Kurt Lewin used the analogy of ice block to explain the concept of change management, which is relevant in almost every area where change is necessary. His model outlines three stages of change management: *Unfreeze – change – Refreeze*.

For example, you've got a cube of ice instead of a cone shape. What you do is change the form by working the ice through stages (changes) that convert it to the shape of your choice. By *unfreezing*, you melt (*change*) the ice cube and then mold it to a cone shape, and then *freeze* it. The significance of this model is embracing change by understanding why the change is necessary in the first instance.

According to Lewin, *"Motivation for change must be generated before change can occur. One must be helped to re-examine many cherished assumptions about oneself and one's relations to others."*[2]

By *unfreezing*, you take the risk, *challenge* status quo, and *prove* the assumptions and underlying behaviors. You are implied to have prepared for the consequences of your choice of *unfreezing* by making further choices to defend what you want from them. By *unfreezing*, you challenge yourself or an organization to re-examine what is hitherto cherished as sacrosanct. In this regard, strategic, cognitive and communication skills are needed.

Change is a process which may take a longer time to achieve its efficacies. Therefore, expect oppositions, challenges, actions, and counteractions as you or people may behave differently. ***Change is like weather; its arrival doesn't meet everyone's expectations. Do not expect the lovers of status quo to embrace it.*** Therefore, develop negotiation and communications skills to effectively manage the ensuing changes.

Refreezing is where personal or organizational goals and programs are implemented, internalized, or institutionalized. Roles are assigned and defined, performance objectives stated, and commitment, disciplines and rewards are effectively communicated.

Remember that failure is an event and success is never final. Failure that is effectively managed and success that is moderately celebrated are precursors to further choices that make further changes inevitable.

CHANGE YOUR MIND

I know a change of mind is perhaps one of the most difficult choices and change preparation that most people are reluctant to make. But a change of mind in a positive direction is necessary to make your dream a reality.

One of the hardest things for humanity is a change of mindset because once a mindset is changed, value change becomes inevitable. And a value change is a product of a personal change.

To be clear, everything is wrong with the culture of inflexibility that smacks of brazen arrogance in the face of growing need for self-improvement, societal upgrade, national transformation, and global overhaul of what's not making us better humans that we're meant to be. A culture that's not making us better as a people must be changed to accommodate modesty and moderate sense of humanity, at least.

Change is a risk. I agree. However, not changing is riskier in the sense that **inflexible people cannot grow or appreciate the growing flavor of humanity because they've refused to learn new things and experience a better side of humanity that can only come to flexible minds.** People with change-resistant mindset would rather indulge or engage in vices such as murders, violence and antisocial activities that demote their societies to a *Hobbesian* state of nature where life is short, brutish, and nasty.

The danger is that, when one has a warped perspective of social orders, or life itself, other peoples' lives wouldn't matter any more than mere objects that can be subjugated at will, to conform to one's whims and caprices – a state of life in utter darkness that is worse than medieval ages.

Ephesians 5:8-9 says, "For though once your heart was full of darkness, now it is full of light from the Lord, and your behavior should show it! Because of this light within you, you should do only what is good and right and true." (TLB).

> Walking in the light begins with an enlightened mind which cannot come without a change of mind.

BEWARE OF DREAM KILLERS

The jungle is a cruel world of the wild. I recently watched a video where the crocodile dragged a deer into murky water. The crocodile glued its cruel teeth to the deer's neck until the latter surrendered in death. The waterside was a comfortable arena for the crocodile while the dry ground was a marathon pitch for the deer.

Most times that's what dream killers and negative company do to you – they drag you into their familiar messy ground where they could ruin your life and thereafter leave you physically or metaphorically dead. They siphon the best part of you – your vision, dreams, focus, energies, and inspirations – and leave you empty. *They drag you into their mud and eventually prevent you from moving on your level ground of strength and stability.* Beware of them at all possible costs!

Dream killers are those people who kill your dreams for whatever reasons. You are as rich as your company. But when you have dream killers around you, you get drained and left with nothing to live for. Do not worry if they leave you because they are necessary losses in life, and you've got to lose the sight of a shoreline to discover new oceans. You've got a dream to live for and a giant to slay but as long as you still mill around dream killers, fulfilment of your dreams becomes elusive.

I believe that your potential, not your current weaknesses, should be your "routing guidance", and when you come across people who want to limit what you could be, to their false perception of your current struggles, you've got to look elsewhere for guidance.

When dream killers want to leave your life, please let them go; after all, your life wasn't any better when you were with them. A Yoruba proverb says that *"a slim tree that cannot support you, cannot kill you when it falls on you!"*

Negative people are toxic. They spoil every good thing in and around you. "As dead flies cause even a bottle of perfume to stink, so a little foolishness spoils great wisdom and honor." Eccl 10:1 (NLT).

In essence, the story of David teaches that, to have victory over unending cycle of frustration and afflictions, you must consciously choose to eliminate naysayers from around you, just as you do the same to negative thoughts and voices, in your mind.

NEGATIVE MENTORS

Do not expect negative voices and thoughts to come from an imagined devil – a masked entity in black robe with more than one horn in the head, and with baritone voice.

Sometimes, negative forces in voices would come from the people that you look up to and respect. This comes so that you believe that your dream is not possible because an important person of King Saul's status - a respected uncle, business mogul, parent, your Professor, Pastor, Prophet, and Bishop - told you to back out.

I read the biography of Malcom X and came across what his teacher told him when he said he wanted to be a lawyer in the future. His teacher said, "We all here like you, you know that. But you've got to be realistic about being a nigger."

A teacher is supposed to be an influencer, a model who should get the best from your worst to guide you to your best. However, Malcom X' teacher continued, "A lawyer-that's no realistic goal for a nigger. You need to think about something you can be. You're good with your hands. Why don't you plan on carpentry?"[3]

Getting unstuck might make you neglect your mentor's counsel and reject the counsel of the most respected personality. Your purpose in life is yours, not your mentor's, not your friends', and not even your parents', frankly!

Avoid negative people as you would a plague!

DON'T WAIT FOR PERFECT CONDITIONS

It's good to make perfect choices. But if you must wait till you get things right before making choices, frustration and indecision may set in. You're not likely to be perfect as a human being, so why would you expect a perfect time for a perfect choice except when it's God speaking?

Mistakes are part of life and if you know how to handle them, you'll succeed despite them.

If David had to wait until he knew all about Goliath, or until he justified himself before the Israelites that he was innocent of Eliab's accusations, or until he got the approval of all his family members, he would not have chosen to confront a champion of 9'9" height. Ecclesiastes 11:4 says, "If you wait for perfect conditions, you will never get anything done." (TLB).

DON'T GAMBLE WITH FEAR

In one of his motivational speeches, Les Brown told his audience a story of a man who was always scared by a bulldog anytime he was going out[3]. It had become repeated episodes for the man to run away each time the dog moved in his direction until one day when the dog got so close to him unawares and he decided to confront the dog head on. A closer look at the dog gave the man the shocker of his life - the bulldog was toothless.

You should never allow fear to motivate your choice lest you get enmeshed in consequential mistakes that can get you irrevocably stuck.

> Fear comes from an unsettled mind and the product of an unsettled mind is an unsettled life.

No one desires to make premature decisions and live the rest of his life in regrets.

Like vengeance, fear has no foresight. Once it takes root in your mind, and bears fruit in your choices, you continue to encounter different manifestations of fear in each of your further choices. *And what value is left in a life that's daily bedeviled with different strokes of fear if not fearful and settled hopeless expectation of death?*

When you are no longer afraid of death, what else can life threaten you with? Research has in fact proven that a greater percentage of our initial fears don't come to pass eventually. This reminds me of an old story that I heard many years ago. When a woman was being pursued by a mad dog, she jumped over a 4ft wall that she'd always seen as a big barrier.

It's instructive to note that once the cause of fear is acted upon, the threat of fear evaporates with time. There's a momentum that is powered by amazing enthusiasm that is daring in its action and efficacious in outcome. You no longer see obstacles as such but as a mere climbing pedestals to reach your goals.

Les Brown was afraid of taking winning actions because he had allowed what others had labeled him – educable mentally retarded student – to limit him, until one day when a teacher called Mr. Washington asked him to write something on the board. "But I can't do it", said Brown. The teacher further asked, "Why not?", to which Brown responded, "Because I am educable mentally retarded." Then Mr. Washington cautioned him, "Don't ever say that again. Someone's opinion of you does not have to become your reality."

That statement liberated him from fears - fear of failure, "What if I fail?" and fear of success, "what if I can't handle it?". This is the same Les Brown who is arguably the best motivational speaker of the twentieth century with multiple awards and recognitions globally.

Fear enslaves indeed. Don't be captured by it!

WISDOM IN CHOICES

I believe we should wrap up our discussion on choice this way: choose wisely.

In your choices, I want to encourage you to be properly guided on when to pause, insist, stop, or decide not to choose in certain situations. The Bible says, "The beginning of wisdom is: Get [skillful and godly] wisdom [it is preeminent] ..." (Prov 4:7, AMP). Wisdom is thus a principal factor in making choices.

I believe the word "Get" could be interpreted to be to "choose" out of the various options. It is important to let wisdom guide in your choices. Good (godly) wisdom begins with fear of God. A man with godly wisdom will mostly, if not always, make choices that reflect fear of God.

I am yet to see a choice that was made from fear of God that is immoral or criminal because "The fear of the LORD is the beginning of wisdom..." (Prov 9:10).

In wisdom you choose the path of honor rather than dishonor; you make choices that glorify God. As in David's case, the voice of wisdom guides you to say NO to limiting choices and encourages you to choose victory instead of defeats. *A choice motivated by wisdom prepares you for attendant challenges as it arms you with capacity to handle changes that come as the offshoots of your initial choices.*

In Genesis 27:38-39, Esau insisted that his father, Isaac, should bless him after he realized that Isaac had blessed Jacob in his stead. While it's not wrong to insist on getting what is meant for you, wisdom will guide to know when, and how to ask. Wisdom will guide whether to pause and examine the contexts, demeanors, and general circumstances.

We are not sure whether Esau studied Isaac's demeanor to know whether insistence on him being blessed at that time was the best decision. Perhaps he should have allowed wisdom to prevail in his request rather than being insistent. The fact that a thing is right does not mean that the timing is equally right. Esau got dangerous set of curses instead of blessings.

A few pages back, we talked about how the so-called *prodigal son* used cognitive self-change for mental redirection. Can you resonate with his cognitive self-change? Does his story describe you or your condition? Have you crossed the boundary with your heavenly father, God?

Have you made fatal mistakes that are now hunting your steps? Now unsure of what the future holds? A similar mental redirection will assure that you are a child of your heavenly father and not a vagabond.

Please join me in singing a stanza in Philip Paul Bliss ageless hymn:

"Though I forget Him and wander away,
Still He doth love me whenever I stray;
Back to His dear loving arms would I flee,
When I remember that Jesus loves me."[5]

You can make the first step in wise choices now; arise and be welcomed to your heavenly father's dear loving arms. Hallelujah! What a way to get unstuck!

Choice is what we think we need first and we act, but wisdom is what we really need before making choices because a choice that ultimately leads to success is the one that is influenced by godly wisdom.

David was not comfortable with the status quo. Are you?

Choose wisdom first and enjoy the consequences of your choices lest you spend the rest of your life serving the consequences of your choices in the barren fields of pain, full of blames and regrets.

You will succeed!

6

SONGS OF TESTIMONY OR FOAMS OF FEAR?

Practicing the Law of Testimony

"And David said unto Saul, thy servant kept his father's sheep, and there came a lion, and a bear, and took a lamb out of the flock: And I went out after him, and smote him, and delivered it out of his mouth: and when he arose against me, I caught him by his beard, and smote him, and slew him. Thy servant slew both the lion and the bear: and this uncircumcised philistine shall be as one of them, seeing he hath defied the armies of the living God."

- I Sam 17:34-36

In some cultures, across the world, getting pregnant and childbearing are the next most important things for women when they get married to. For a woman who really wants kids, anything short of that is a *big deal* and if she's a Christian, that would be the most undesirable "trial of faith" experience. In those cultures, nothing Compares to the pain, shame, and ridicule associated with barrenness.

Bouts of doubts. The womb is empty while the heart is heavy. Hissing rapidly like a vexed snake; mouth opening intermittently with no words coming out. Pacing back and forth with no target actions. Talking to self like a mentally deranged, answering "yes" when no one is calling, and smiling while hot tears court down her face. Getting angry at nothing. She spits out, but not like a woman who's missed her period. It's a mixture of saliva and tasty tears that have marked her face, from eyes to chin, and then to every part of her body.

She's not sweating; and when she happens to, it's the mixture of tears and sweats that get her soaked. Insomnia? Yes, what else do you expect from a woman who'd made realities out of teddy bears and pillows?

Indeed, heavy metal proves to be of feather weight compares to the burden of childlessness. *"Is this an anathema?"*, *"Did anyone curse me?"*, *"What did I do wrong?"*, *"What if I'm barren, really?"* These are some of the probing questions in the mind of an agitated woman who's desperately in search of a child!

The last thing in her mind is a question: *"is this God's will for me at this time?"*

Christy Ogbeide was no exception to these ordeals that she had to contend with, not long after her marriage. Christy got married to Emmanuel Ogbeide in 1979 brimming with hope of being a mother nine months after. But this was not to be until 14 years after! She neither planned for this nor thought about it since her mother had seven children. "After the doctor completed several different tests and examinations, he told me it appeared that I would have difficulty having a baby, and that it may not happen at all. The test results indicated that I have big cyst on the left side of my ovaries", she said.

She then started treatments and got pregnant in 1981. "Unfortunately, tragedy struck at the fifth month of the pregnancy and we lost the baby girl", she added, with a tone of desperation. This was a big challenge to a 23-year-old woman who had a good salvation relationship with Jesus Christ. She likened her experience to a "fiery ordeal" which Apostle Peter talked about in I Peter 4:12.

After that terrible experience, Christy relocated to the United States where she pursued higher education till Ph.D. level, not wanting in Christ stewardship services. Her faith waxed stronger even as she continued to be a blessing to others in the face of her childless condition.

The high point of her life was when she lived as if her "problems" existed no more. She decided to live in thanksgiving, leveraging on David's attitudes (Ps 50:14-15) and Hannah who made a vow to the Lord when she was desperately in need of a child, (I Sam 1:11), and Jacob who made vows to God. (Gen 28:20-22).

"O Lord my God if you can deliver me from this pain and unknown sickness, I will serve you all of the days of my life", Christy vowed to God.

Suffice to state here that, Christy started doing the unusual, because she was expecting the unusual to happen. She started sharing the testimonies of the goodness of God. Even though she was medically adjudged to be unlikely to be a mother, she was telling all that cared to listen, that she was soon to be a mother.

Meanwhile in the past, she had to avoid baby sections in the grocery shops as that would remind her of her pains of childlessness. "… in my life whenever I went to the store, I purposely would go past the area where baby things were displayed, and start thanking God that very soon I would also be buying those things", she said.

When you are expecting great things to happen, it's important to align the state of your mind with your expectations, living in the reality of your expectations, and openly demonstrate it for others to see, especially a demonstration of faith. In this way, you'll be well poised to receive the physical blessings.

Christy went on: "And, of course in this condition, my body

changed in just few months…When the going got tough, I danced for hours praising God and glorifying His ever living name."[1]

She had done IVF four times and had given up on whatever promises that came with a promise of another IVF. But it eventually happened in 1992 when she gave birth to Joshua Ogbeide – the miracle baby Joshua.

Finally, she said, "Giving thanks for what you have not received keeps you focused and strengthens your faith. It encourages you to keep your hopes high. It keeps your mind at rest and challenges God to prove Himself in your life."[2]

Pastor Christy's mourning turned into dancing, and her hitherto morbid frame of heart cheered with songs of joy. A new day dawned. The heavy sullen cloud that used to dissolve into empty winds and icy weather around her now lets out the showers of blessings for which she continues to testify.

THE LAW OF TESTIMONY

The word "testimony" has more than one meaning. Legally speaking, it may mean oral or written evidence of a witness in support of a case or cause. In religious setting, a testimony is a narration of an experience (of God's goodness). In the context of this chapter, the latter definition is preferred.

The law of testimony states that *a man's testimony is a gratitude expressed, and the prophecy of God's abilities and possibilities waiting to be manifested in the future*. The testimony of past experiences shows that you are not an ingrate.

Yes, your testimonies are prophecies to your future! A testimony recounted potentially assures future possibilities because the words or promises of God that produced the variables of the current testimonies are constant. Hebrews 13:8 says, "Jesus Christ the same yesterday, and today, and forever." (KJV). Jesus is the Word. (See John 1:1).

THE MIRACLE OF TESTIMONY

Miracles are man's experiences of God's interventions that are illogical and defy known principles.

The miracle of constantly recounting the past experiences of God's goodness is manifold. It is an expression of gratitude. It's an evangelism. It births hope and future assurances - *if God did that in the past, then he can do it again, and even more*. In addition, the law of testimony ignites encouragement which is an important factor in the quest for success.

Hope births encouragement which is the mother of winning actions. Romans 5:5 says, "Such hope [in God's promises] never disappoints *us*, because God's love has been abundantly poured out within our hearts through the Holy Spirit who was given to us." (AMP).

For example, a patient who's diagnosed with a particular disease would normally get encouraged on hearing that someone with similar medical conditions was cured. This encouragement would jolt the patient to take his medicine regularly, pray intensely, and take more pro-recovery steps believing in the possibility that he too can recover. This gingers the patient to sing for joy even in his afflictions. Yes, you read that right - singing for joy in afflictions because of hope. That's why it's called the miracle of testimonies.

The testimonies that you recounted is not only benefitting you but also others who listen and get encouraged and receive guidance for future experiences. You may be thinking: *does God have to repeat himself? What if He changes His ways or manners? Why would anyone depend on the past events for inspiration for future actions?*

Well, you might be right in some ways, at least, logically speaking.

101

> But syllogism is far from being abso-
> lute when you're relating with God,
> or when you're expecting something
> from God because He is all-powerful,
> having all the means and depending
> on nothing - including logics and na-
> ture.

Yet, nothing exists or survives outside of Him. *He doesn't have to repeat himself in a particular way to bless you. He can choose to create many other ways to bless you.*

THE SAME GOD, DIFFERENT TESTIMONIES

The emphasis under the law of testimony is not much of *what He did* in the past but *the principle behind His actions for which we testify.* Even if He changes His ways and manners, His principles do not change. To be sure, like the Israelites, *anyone who must depend only on past events for inspiration for future, has little or no knowledge of God or His principles.*

Our experiences do change and even sometimes people often exaggerate their experiences with fictions to embellish them hoping that they'll be more credible. That is man. But not with God who doesn't change. When we hang on to God's sure promises as we testify of His past *gifts to us,* a sure hope surges from within us to make us fight with focus. That is why the Bible assures us:

> "To those who were to receive what he promised, God
> wanted to make it very clear that he would never change
> his purpose; so he added his vow to the promise. There are
> these two things, then, that cannot change and about which

God cannot lie. So we who have found safety with him are greatly encouraged to hold firmly to the hope placed before us."

- Heb 6:17-18 (GNT)

David's Testimonies

Before David's historic physical fight with Goliath, he engaged in a lot of confessions that were inspirational and testified about his past experiences from where he drew strength and enthusiasm. His testimonies were not abstract, vague hypocritical expressions of make-beliefs but phenomenal encounters of escapes from dangers which could not have happened except with God's help:

- thy servant kept his father's sheep,
- there came a lion, and a bear,
- and took a lamb out of the flock:
- And I went out after him,
- smote him, and delivered it out of his mouth:
- when he arose against me,
- I caught him by his beard,
- and smote him, and slew him.
- Thy servant slew both the lion and the bear

Did you notice this unique pattern of episodes elsewhere in I Samuel 17? We will talk more about these under the law of action. As you can see, these testimonies recounted by David in verses 34 and 35 are followed by similar patterns in verse 48 to 51 where he eventually severed Goliath's head from his body.

What does this tell you? *The testimony you confidently and repeatedly share is waiting to replicate itself sooner or later.* The similar strategy that David used to kill bear and lion, was the one he used to kill Goliath.

TRIUMPH BY TESTIMONIES

Apart from the fact that confessing possibilities in the face of seeming impossibilities is a victory, singing songs of testimonies energizes your spirit being which builds up your spiritual formidability against satanic oppositions.

Satan has been fighting against good causes since when he rebelled and was expelled from God's presence, and unless resisted, he would continue to compete with your success. In Revelations chapter 12, we read about the great dragon who wanted to snatch a newborn male child from his mother; but he failed. This dragon represented the devil or Satan while the newborn male child referred to Jesus Christ who would rule with iron scepter.

Then a great war ensued between Angel Michael and his co-angels on one side and the dragon and *his* angels on the other. The dragon side lost the battle and was banished from the heaven to the earth. How did Angel Michael and his company win the Satan? They triumphed by the power in the blood of the lamb and testimony of the word.

Blood of the Lamb – Revelations 12:11 says in part, "And they overcame *and* conquered him because of the blood of the Lamb…" (AMP). In the Bible, Jesus is referred to as the Lamb of God. Lamb is naturally mild, quiet, obedient, and not confrontational. This typified Jesus Christ even when He had all powers to escape the imminent substitutive death.

"He was oppressed, and he was afflicted, yet he opened not his mouth: he is brought as a lamb to the slaughter, and as a sheep before her shearers is dumb, so he openeth not his mouth." (Is 53:7). When John the Baptist saw Jesus coming to him, described Jesus this way, "Behold the Lamb of God, which taketh away the sin of the world." (Jn 1:29).

Jesus hanged on the tree, shed his blood, died, and resurrected to *purchase* for us the salvation from sin and all that entered the world with it. (See Hebrews 9:14, 12:24; Acts 20:28; Revelation 1:5; I Corinthians 6:20; Matthew 26:28).

The significance of the triumph by the *blood of the Lamb* is primarily in the forgiveness of our sins and a change of our status from *vagabond sinners* to *adopted children*. (I Jn 3:1-5). According to Paul, "… we are convinced of better things concerning you, and of things that accompany salvation." (Heb 6:9, AMP). Other benefits that accompanied our salvation range from good (divine) health, success, victory, to long life, joy, and peaceful life.

Your experiences of triumph, success, and blessings that come from salvation in Jesus Christ become more and more real in practical terms when you testify (speak) of your *salvation* experiences especially in the face of life obstacles. This testimony is a motivation not only for you but also for others.

The angels who cast devil down to the earth in defeat overcame by the saving power of God in the blood Jesus. This power was not just in their knowledge but in the verbal expressions met with prompt, God-directed actions. The result was victory.

Word of testimonies – Revelations 12:11 partly states, "And they overcame him by … by the word of their testimony…" This means that Angel Michael and his colleagues got unstuck not because they knew God's words nor because they remembered the goodness of God, but because God's grace that manifested in the form of Word that was in their lips – they testified what God did in the past and what His words says He would do.

I can figure Angel Michael speaking authoritatively, *"Listen you foul dragon, 'For it is written, "As I live," says the Lord, "every knee shall bow to me and every tongue confess to God." (Rom 14:11: Is 45:23). Because you have failed to bow to the most high God, we declare your place empty in heaven. And because you have refused to confess and acknowledge*

God, you are hereby cast out to the earth…" Because the angels testified of the will of God, the obstacles gave way.

The principles behind God's faithfulness and goodness to us that became our testimonies are His words which are either *logos (the written word)* as written in the Bible or *rhema (the revealed word)* as otherwise spoken or communicated for specific instructions. Psalm 119:89 says, "Forever, oh Lord, thy Word is settled in heaven."

The integrity of God's words makes for His reliability because He "…doesn't change like the shifting shadows produced by the sun and the moon." (James 1:17, GW).

David was a warrior for most part of his lifetime and God gave him victory everywhere. This was possible because God surrounded him with songs of deliverance. Psalm 32:7 says, "Thou art my hiding place; thou shall preserve me from trouble, thou shall compass me about with songs of deliverance." Check out the Easy-to-Read Version which says, "… So I sing about the way you saved me." (ERV*)*. David literally sang his testimonies.

DON'T REPLACE SONGS OF TESTIMONIES WITH SONGS OF SORROW

Perhaps one of the most illustrative scenarios where many people, and I guess including you and me, keep sealed lips in respite and throw in the towel, is when confronted with obstacles that seemingly defy solutions.

Think of intractable diseases and sicknesses, facing foreclosures, constant cycle of failures, painful divorce, loss of all retirement benefits, being told by physicians that you have few weeks to live, or specifically being in David's condition when he was often trapped in life and death situations.

> If you can keep your shoulders high, call good days to mind, and sing songs of testimonies like David, you'll keep hope alive.

Keeping hope alive in some instances may mean to not stop positive actions because you hope to win. Remember, "Such hope [in God's promises] never disappoints *us...*" (Rom 5:5, AMP).

David often recounted his testimonies as a habit in the form of Psalms: "You have turned my mourning into dancing for me; You have taken off my sackcloth and clothed me with joy, that my soul may sing praise to You and not be silent. O LORD my God, I will give thanks to You forever." (Ps 30:11-12, AMP).

Every living person has songs of testimonies. Do not lose your songs to foams of fear or songs of sorrow.

KEEP HOPE ALIVE!

I want you to follow me to Psalm 137. But before then, carefully read the lines following from Nehemiah 1:1-4.

The words of Nehemiah the son of Hachaliah. And it came to pass in the month Chisleu, in the twentieth year, as I was in Shushan the palace, That Hanani, one of my brethren, came, he and certain men of Judah; and I asked them concerning the Jews that had escaped, which were left of the captivity, and concerning Jerusalem.

And they said unto me, The remnants that are left of the captivity there in the province are in great affliction and reproach: the wall of Jerusalem also is broken down, and the gates thereof are burned with fire.

And it came to pass, when I heard these words, that I sat down and wept, and mourned certain days, and fasted, and prayed before the God of heaven."

This is a story of the Jews when they were taken captive into the foreign land where they had lost their liberty to the enemies. Their homes in Jerusalem were in ruins which blurred the possibility of happy life upon return, if ever. They could not do what they wanted to do. Their choices, if ever, were limited. They lived in fear of the unknown. Their lives were little costlier than those of the livestock of their Babylonian captors. Their past was nothing to write home about even as their future became increasingly bleak by each passing day.

BY THE RIVERS OF BABYLON...

Do the Israelites servitude experiences describe your conditions? These experiences were captured in Psalm 137:1-4 which reads:

> "By the rivers of Babylon, There we [captives] sat down and wept, When we remembered Zion [the city God imprinted on our hearts]. On the willow trees in the midst of Babylon We hung our harps. For there they who took us captive demanded of us a song with words, And our tormentors [who made a mockery of us demanded] amusement, *saying*, "Sing us one of the songs of Zion." How can we sing the LORD'S song in a strange and foreign land?" (AMP)

These Israelites' negative experiences of failures in the hands of their captors immobilized them and consequently affected their ways of thinking. *"How can we sing the Lord's song in a strange and foreign land?"*, they asked.

What happened to their knowledge that the earth is the Lord's and its fullness thereof? Why did they forget that God had said that He is the Lord of all flesh? That He is the Lord and that there's no other God?

Why did they soon forget that the God of Israel is the God of heavens and of the depths? Why did they fail to recall these "words of testimonies" and sing them, even in the face of oppressions and afflictions?

Their forefathers saw the red sea parted and Jordan bifurcated. They and their fathers had seen Ai hounded, destroyed and Amalekites mowed like grass. For example, the Bible says, "After the victory, the LORD instructed Moses, "Write this down on a scroll as a permanent reminder and read it aloud to Joshua: I will erase the memory of Amalek from under heaven." (Ex 17:14, NLT).

> Unlike David, the Israelites' morbid film of blankness that had eclipsed their past chirpy experiences of rejoicing in Jerusalem dissolved into bubbles of negative expressions and grasshopper mentality.

Their hitherto happy countenances got evaporated in the face of bitter experiences of slavery. They did not see any reason to rejoice and sing. These were the people who had every reason to call to mind, all the goodness of the Lord to them and rejoice with songs of testimony.

They did not bring testimonies out of their wonderful experiences of God's protections but foams of fear, songs of sorrow and roars of regrets, and that's why getting unstuck was difficult for them.

Please don't be like them.

SINGING OUT YOUR TESTIMONIES IN THE STRANGE LAND!

Your negative experiences may be strange but not to God. Besides, there's no strange land before God. God owns the mountains just as He owns the valleys and islands. He owns the oceans and seas and all that is in them. He knows the right keys to all doors and has the correct codes to all locks. His has the hearts of the kings in His hands. He can do and undo. That's why He's God!

Change the worldview of your challenge. You can still sing out in the face of strange situations!

Unlike Jacob who raised *bethel* out of his stony grief, the captive Israelites sang songs of sorrow from their experiences of horror, raising no *bethel* but *mountains* of complaints.

Your strange condition may be barrenness, debts, bad credit, wayward kids, failing exams or some sorts of spiritual battles with some unseen forces that have now crippled your life and halted your businesses. Sing out God's abilities anyway!

Is it miscarriages, or a protracted illness? Sing out. Don't be like the Israelites in Babylon who refused to sing out the past goodness of God when they said, *"How can we sing the Lord's song in a strange land?"*.

David once said, "The earth is the LORD's, and the fullness of it, the world, and those who dwell in it. For He has founded it upon the seas and established it upon the streams *and the rivers.*" (Ps 24:1-2, AMP).

The Israelites' experiences in Psalm 137:1-4 above sharply contrast with David's in I Samuel 17:34-36. David said, "Thy servant slew both the lion and the bear: and this uncircumcised philistine shall be as one of them, seeing he hath defied the armies of the living God." (I Sam 17:36).

This song of testimony was replicated when David severed Goliath's head from his body. Songs of testimony are powerful tools in getting you unstuck.

TESTIFYING BY FAITH

I believe we should wrap us with this.

The law of testimony is an expression of faith and is motivated by hope. Testimonies in our context are not limited to past experiences but extend to confessions of what you hope for, and which is rooted in God's words or promises. This is a testimony of what you believe God is saying about your obstacles, even when it looks stupid to others who are possibly limited by human senses. We would consider two biblical examples.

Let's start with John the Baptist. John 1:6-8 reads: "There came a man commissioned *and* sent from God, whose name was John. This man came as a witness, to testify about the Light, so that all might believe [in Christ, the Light] through him. John was not the light, but came to testify about the Light." (AMP).

John started testifying before Jesus Christ was born because he believed God who promised to send His son to the world. That was enough to testify about.

The second character is Abraham. Many years passed between the time of God's promise and manifestation concerning the birth of Isaac. During this time frame, a lot had happened, including discouragement and distractions. "But Abraham never doubted. He believed God, for his faith and trust grew ever stronger, and he praised God for this blessing even before it happened." (Rom 14:20, TLB).

What empowered Abraham to praise God in bad time? *He praised God for this blessing even before it happened.* This was his testimony that stemmed from faith. "He was completely sure that God was well able to do anything he promised." (v. 21). Abraham's testimony of God's ability to fulfil His promise expressed in faith, made God to forgive "his sins and declared him "not guilty." (v. 22).

111

When you appreciate God and confess His name in testimony of His past goodness, you provoke His power to save you. Psalm 50:23 says, "Whoever offers praise glorifies Me; And to him who orders *his* conduct *aright* I will show the salvation of God." (NKJV). When you testify to what is not yet in existence (like John the Baptist), and your testimony is rooted in God's will and promise (like Abraham), you provoke God into action because God's "bond" is His word. So, either way, your sincere testimonies are certain ways to get you unstuck.

Abraham testified of God's abilities by praising Him, and he later became the Father of Isaac. David testified of God's goodness in appreciation, and of what his God would do to his obstacle (Goliath). Then his obstacle became history.

Chrsity Ogbeide was full of testimonies of God's creative ability even when she was barren for many years. But eventually, she became a mother.

In the context of this chapter, it's not yet a testimony if it's only in your mind – not until when it's shared or verbally expressed. Your obstacles will become history and grounds for future testimonies!

Amen!

7

ASSURANCE OF VICTORY

Amplification of the Law of Faith

"Thy servant slew both the lion and the bear: and this uncircumcised Philistine shall be as one of them, seeing he hath defied the armies of the living God."

"David said moreover, The LORD that delivered me out of the paw of the lion, and out of the paw of the bear, he will deliver me out of the hand of this Philistine. And Saul said unto David, Go, and the LORD be with thee."

-I Sam 17:36-37

I remember as law school students, we were taught that the best route to a successful legal writing – especially in writing answers to essay questions – is either the CIRAC (Conclusion, Issues, Rule, Analysis and Conclusion) or IRAC (Issues, Rule, Analysis and Conclusion) method. Some professors (especially who are also examiners) would advise that, CIRAC is better because it allows the examiner to know whether the examinee knows the answer in the first place, when the examinee starts with the conclusion.

Hypothetically, an examinee may be asked whether Tom's statement in a given context, is likely to be admitted in evidence. A good example of drawing a conclusion from the outset looks like this: *"Tom's statement may not be admitted in evidence because it is hearsay and does not fall within any exception to the hearsay rule."*

Once you conclude correctly right away, it becomes more likely than not, that you would generally have higher chance of success in the essay because the examiner would go through the rest of your answers with the mindset that you know what you're talking about.

Using the law of faith to get unstuck works the same way. *The best way to fight and win is to draw a conclusion of victory before beginning the task. By this, you've dovetailed your energies to one thing – victory! This gives you a sense of focus and discipline, knowing that, even when the battle is tougher than anticipated and your energy is draining, you already knew that it's victory or nothing.*

David drew a conclusion of victory over Goliath before he began the physical combat, saying "and this uncircumcised Philistine shall be as one of them, seeing he hath defied the armies of the living God." (I Sam 17:37).

THE LAW OF FAITH

The law of faith states that *you take a winning step, including having a mental picture of its reality, not because you are currently experiencing a desired victory but because you believe that's what would happen when you act.*

Faith is an assurance and evidence. That's why Hebrews 11:1 says, "Now faith is the assurance (title deed, confirmation) of things hoped for (divinely guaranteed), and the evidence of things not seen (the conviction of their reality – faith comprehends as fact what cannot be experienced by physical senses]." (AMP).

Because of your *assurance* that your action would bring results, you then take steps, and this is an *evidence* of the reality of the fruits of your action. Before David's eventual action that killed Goliath, he already got the *evidence*: "*... this uncircumcised Philistine shall be as one of them...*" The word "shall" in most cases, connotes a mandatory expression which means that David's evidence of Goliath's defeat was very real – he was convinced of the reality of Goliath's elimination. That's faith!

When David told Goliath that he (Goliath) would be like the lion and bear that he (David) killed, David had not physically fought with Goliath. When he told the giant that God would deliver him (giant) into his hand, Goliath's global title then was "the Champion".

This tells you that it does not matter the size of the mountain of problems before you, neither is the medical diagnosis on you. *What matters is the conclusion of victory in your heart at any given time.*

What is faith?

Faith looks at a thing the way God looks at it – a done deal! Faith looks at a thing from the possibility that, because God-directed steps have been taken, victory is sure. Faith says, *"because God is in this with me, I am taking this step and I will succeed"*. This is what ancient people, including David, were commended for. (See Hebrews 11:32-33).

I believe that Abraham took steps to slaughter his only son, believing that *"even if Isaac's head is severed from his body, God can make Isaac to be alive again, because it was God who asked me to take the step."* God told Abraham that he would become the father of many nations. Abraham set out, not knowing the details yet. That is faith in its most practical sense. Faith in action! He heard God's direction for his future and did not sit back or stand akimbo.

Faith is different from mere mental assent!

Faith is not a mental assent

I have heard and seen many people, including Christians, relying on mere mental assent assuming that they have faith. Of course, that's why many of us still don't have what we're "faithing", even after a lot of jamborees and activities that we mistake for *stewardship services in God's vineyards.*

What is mental assent? This is a mere positive acquiescence that *"things will happen anyways since God knows all things and can do all things"* without more. Mental assent cannot move an ant let alone lynching the giant like Goliath. It's like a brand-new AK-47 without rams of ammunition. Such powerful weapon is reduced to a mere chunky wood.

> People with mental assent rarely take pro-active actions but keep confessing and hoping that one day, things would get better.

They are complacent, hoping that "anything can happen." Yes, anything can happen but certainly not "everything good and worthwhile" thing, which is the product of focused, God-inspired actions.

When you divorce word-inspired actions from the meaning of faith in God what is left is mental assent because the latter feeds on mental calculations and permutations.

A person with a mere mental assent sits down, crosses his legs, and keeps saying, "All is well…" because the Bible says, "All is well".

Practical Faith - *A man of practical faith stands up, keeps working toward solutions, and would not stop saying what he believes would happen — "all is well…" - even when his current experiences prove otherwise.*

In II Kings 4, a Shunammite woman's only son (miracle son) was with his father in the farm, suddenly held his head in pain and died. I pray you never have to experience this sorrow. When an only son dies, it is unthinkable how his mother would behave. However, she didn't lose her spiritual sense.

I guess she must have reasoned, *"The son came because Prophet Elisha prayed for me. Even so now I must go to the same man of God to tell him that the boy is dead so that he can do whatever he can. Maybe it would have been better if I were without one than to have experienced the joy of motherhood for a while and then suddenly, no more."*

But to be sure she wanted her son back desperately in real terms and not a mere wishful thinking, **she stepped out.** Not only that, when she was asked whether all was well, **she was sure to match her actions and expectations with her words**: "All is well." (V. 26, NKJV). That's faith in a practical way!

CONCLUSION OF VICTORY FROM THREE HEBREW MEN

The Bible's story of Shadrach, Meshach, and Abednego (the three Hebrew men) presents a classical example of the amplification of the law of faith. These men had more than a giant before them – the draconian decree, the king, some accusing Chaldeans, and death by blazing fire.

King Nebuchadnezzar had decreed that whoever would not bow down to the golden statute in the plain of Dura located in the province of Babylon would be thrown into a furnace of blazing fire. (Daniel 3:6). It was like the whole world was against them.

Rather than resign to fate, the three Hebrew men amplified the law of faith; they drew a conclusion of victory from the onset.

According to them, "If we are thrown into the flaming furnace, our God is able to deliver us; and he will deliver us out of your hand, Your Majesty. But if he doesn't, please understand, sir, that even then we will never under any circumstance serve your gods or worship the gold statue you have erected." (Dan 3:17-18, TLB).

What a conclusion of faith!

What was the result of the men's conclusion? They were thrown into the furnace, but they came out unscathed; the people "saw that the fire had no effect on the bodies of these men: not a hair of their head was singed, their robes were unaffected, and there was no smell of fire on them." (Dan 3:27, HCSB).

> There is a link between the conclusion of victory from the onset and the ensuing defeat of obstacles and this link is the Spirit of faith.

It may come in form of inspiration or in miracle. Whatever it is, the causative factor is the Spirit of faith in God.

CONCLUSION OF VICTORY FROM DANIEL

Daniel was another classical example of faith in God. This was someone who learnt of the draconian decree meant to persecute him because of his faith in God and value system (praying to the God of Israel rather than pray to Darius within a thirty-day period). He was unwavering and confidently dared his accusers. *Daniel's giant was the misfortune of being thrown into the lions' den* (See Daniel 6:16). His condition was much more precarious because the law was that of Medes and Persian which was irrevocable.

But Daniel's faith in the living God got him unstuck. According to him, "…My God sent his angel, who closed the mouths of the lions so that they would not hurt me. I've been found innocent before God and also before you, O king. I've done nothing to harm you." (Dan 6:21-22, MSG).

His faith in God that *"put him in trouble"* also got him out of the trouble.

THE WISDOM OF FAITH IN GOD

The Hebrew men, Daniel, David, and a host of other generals in the scriptures could not have naturally taken those steps of faith let alone faced and conquered those obstacles. They operated in an unusual realm of faith beyond the abilities or philosophies of men which were not absolute.

Paul encouraged the church in Corinth so that their *"faith would not rest on human wisdom ..."* (I Cor 2:5). When overwhelmed with obstacles, it is a natural human tendency to first look for anything around that is available for immediate solution.

> But we must realize that human wisdom is finite and often flawed and ineffective in addressing novel challenges or when in contest with a person of superior wisdom or higher power.

When your faith however rests on the supernatural wisdom of God, like we see in David when he confronted Goliath, you can't but win the battles of life. To be clear, to have faith in God is wisdom, just as fearing Him. This explains why the heroes of faith chronicled in Hebrews 11, including David, received credit as reward. They had options but decided to move with higher wisdom - faith in God.

Like David, you may have alternatives to an exercise of faith in God. But such alternatives may let you down – whether you are familiar with them or not. David was not familiar with the available alternative of King Saul's armor and rejected it and took steps of faith with which he was familiar. He won!

FAITH IS SUPERNATURAL

By faith, the invisible God created the visible world from what was invisible. This accentuates the reality of the certainty of the supernatural over the natural because the latter is the product of the former. Thus, the supernatural world of faith is wider, broader, and bigger than the natural.

> "By faith [that is, with an inherent trust and enduring confidence in the power, wisdom and goodness of God] we understand that the worlds (universe, ages) were framed and created [formed, put in order, and equipped for their intended purpose] by the word of God, so that what is seen was not made out of things which are visible."
>
> - Heb 11:3, AMP

God was deliberate in making faith to be supernatural because that's who He is and where He dwells – the unlimited invisible. *Your faith in God draws and places demands on the inexhaustible power and ability of God, whereas your senses depend on the limited resources that can be depleted with passage of time or with human errors.*

In creating the world that you see, God "procured" the needed resources from the unseen by the "unlimited world" of faith; he used more than the five senses to which a natural man is limited. Though the five senses may give you something, you need more than five senses to sustain it, for your own good and for posterity.

God believed in himself and spoke into existence, all that He wanted. *If you have faith in Him, then He would make something out of your nothingness. Your faith in God draws on God's all-time abilities that can satisfy your needs at any given time, to fulfill your purpose.* I Chronicle 15:26 says "Because God had helped the Levites who were carrying the ark of the covenant of the LORD, seven bulls and seven rams were sacrificed." (NIV).

You are saying, *"God, I believe you and based on your power, do this for me".* God says, *"I honor my word which formed the basis of your belief and because my word is my bond, I will do it for you in due course."*

It's therefore in the place of God's help that your faith in Him gets you unstuck.

Trusting God in fearful times

The issue is not whether you're going to be fearful but *why*, and *what* you do when confronted with fearful situations. In your calmness and being articulate, your mind works better to produce solutions.

Fears, anxieties, and solutions are strange bedfellows.

In one of David's fearful moments when he was seized by the Philistines in Gath, his reason for fear was understandable. They wanted to kill him. But he told God, "When I am afraid, I will trust in you. In God I trust; I will not be afraid. What can mortal man do to me?" (Ps 56:3-4, NIV). The calming assurance that comes from consciousness of God's help got him out of fear.

I was driving home from work recently and I suddenly had a flat tire (or should I say a burnt tire, because it was like someone had set it on fire). Thankfully, I was not speeding when it happened though I was in the middle lane. Somehow, I managed to get to an exit and then parked beside a nearby street. By this time, it was getting late at night. The neighborhood was purely residential which meant that the possibility of getting help from a nearby tire shop or a mechanic workshop was remote.

I called my wife to let her know my fate. She suggested I call our roadside assistant number. There was no success and then fears started setting in. I put on a smiling face as I entered the car to move it to a better location. I said to myself *"Afterall, the worst that could happen is bad rim"*, as I drove and kept looking out for any "angel" that God might bring my way.

Meanwhile, I couldn't really pray for obvious reasons. After about ten minutes of struggle with the steering (though I was calm within), I entered the car park of what I believed was an elementary school where I met a man who was about to enter his car. He offered to help but his equipment did not fix it, just like mine could not. Now I was almost giving up hope as it was now getting darker with fewer people around. I was determined to dial 911 when I saw a big truck packed before me. I wasted no time in telling him about my greatest need at that time. His equipment could not lose my vehicle's wheel nuts that had become slippery.

Then a guy in company of his girlfriend, quickly made his ways toward me, looked at my wheel briefly and went back to his car. He came back with his impact wrench and instructed me to do nothing but watch. He replaced my tire in less than fifteen minutes. I was speechless but managed to say, "thank you" but he said, "no problem."

I heard his girlfriend say some words in Spanish. Then I said, "Gracias, Gracias!!" since that was the perfect word I could say in Spanish. They both laughed out loud and bid me farewell. Then a surge of ease welled up from the pit of my being as I heard a word from my spirit, "God is our present help in times of trouble...". Hallelujah!

Though I wasn't sure of where the help would come from, I was rest assured that I would get some help. And that's what happened. Glory to God!

The miracle of trusting in God in time of fear is the wonder of His intervention in your affairs. God births certain inspiration in you (enthusiasm) that produces unstoppable passion and energies that propel you to take safe steps. Any devil that messes with you then becomes history. Psalm 34:5 says, "They look to Him and were radiant; their faces will never blush in shame or confusion." (AMP). Goliath was a good example of a victim of God's furious intervention.

> The fact is, if your inner and outer eyes are blinded by fears, then your hands and legs would be paralyzed before dangers. And the longer you're immobilized, the faster you become a victim. That shall not be your portion in Jesus' name.

GROW AND WIN WITH YOUR FAITH

Everyone has faith in one thing or the other. You have faith that your Uber driver would not plunge you into a canal; that your pilot would not crash-land you and that the food in your mouth would not come out from your nose, barring unforeseen accidents. Your faith in all of these developed with time by your experiences, familiarity, and some knowledge about them.

The more familiar and engrossed you are with God's words, the deeper your faith takes root. As you know, the more you communicate with your loved ones, the more you communicate meaningfully, and the more understanding you have of them, and this increases the trust level.

The more you communicate with God through His words, the more you trust Him.

The primary place to develop and grow your faith in God is His words, especially His instructions.

Rom 10:17 says, "So then faith cometh by hearing, and hearing by the word." "Hearing" of God's word here does not only mean the proper functioning of your temporal lobe for auditory purpose. It means that you develop faith in God when constant hearing and absorbing of His word produce an understanding that the best way to live is by trusting and resting on His mightiness and capacity to accomplish His promises.

If hearing of God's word alone brings faith then everyone with auditory cortex who has been hearing God's word would have faith in God. Your faith in God grows when your understanding of His word grows and increases your trust level.

Take notice that faith grows. And do not forget that the faith that grows is the one that is nurtured. God's word is the most authentic means of nurturing your faith unto fruitfulness. Those who can't patiently relate with God by growing through His word would want to get unstuck outside of God's principles. Fewer things in life quickly ground a person to poverty and agony than unreasonable gambles.

Paul told the Corinthian believers that his message of Christ to them, came with demonstration of God's power and not based on rhetoric, so that their "... faith would not rest on the wisdom and rhetoric of men, but on the power of God." (I Cor 2:5, AMP). The power of God (for man's salvation) is in the Word of God that found expression in the Son of God, Jesus Christ. (See Romans 1:16, KJV). Those who base their faith in God's Word don't end in shame!

God is the Word, and the Word is God. The Word changed its form and manifested in human form called Jesus Christ. When you live by the Word, listen to the Word, read the Word, and relate with the Word, you develop your faith in God through the Word, and take Him by His Word. Then you would know His plan for you and not have difficulty believing Him. This is where you begin to get unstuck.

Common sense and spirituality don't always merge! The danger of basing your faith on human wisdom and mere rhetoric is that human wisdom and rhetoric are dithering, dependent on natural factors, and subject to changes. But the faith that sustainably gets you unstuck is the one that rests on God's power (God's words which are eternal) and relents not even in trying times.

"IT DIDN'T HAPPEN; THEREFORE, I DIDN'T HAVE FAITH IN THE FIRST INSTANCE"

Let's begin to conclude our discussions on the law of faith.

You probably can summarize our discussions so far this way: "*You need faith in God to get unstuck because faith will make things happen for you.*"

I tell you that you won't be wrong at all if you conclude this way. But there's more to add. I have come across people, including Pastors and ministers, who believe that once what you're believing God for, didn't happen physically, it means that you either didn't have faith in the first instance or that your faith didn't work. This assertion is not always the case, biblically.

To start with, by Hebrews 11:1, faith is an *evidence* or a *proof* of what is not yet seen. It is being "certain of what we do not see." (NIV). In other words, among other things, at the time you have faith in God, that's when you have evidence of the existence of the thing. And no one worries again whether he would have the thing of which evidence he already has in possession!

Moreover, Hebrews 11:13 says, "All these died in faith [guided and sustained by it], without receiving the [tangible fulfillment of God's] promises, only having seen (anticipated) them and having welcomed them from a distance, and having acknowledged that they were strangers and exiles on the earth." (AMP).

This shows that the beauty of faith is living in and by it (that is, living mentally in the reality of what you're trusting God for) such that your *ultimate* joy doesn't hang on physical happenstances of your expectations.

Oswald Chambers said, *"Seeing is never believing: we interpret what we see in the light of what we believe. Faith is confidence in God before you see God emerging; therefore the nature of faith is that it must be tried…. We have to trust in God whether He sends us money or not, whether He gives us health or not. We must have faith in God, not in his gifts…'"*

I agree to his words because faith is a proof of possession or an evidence of relationship, and this makes living worthwhile, "For we live by faith, not by sight." (II Cor 5:7, NIV).

When you have this mindset, it makes your life journey a pleasant experience in that you wouldn't have to postpone the joy of true living until a certain future happenstance. You would live in the moment with the reality that you have the evidence of that thing NOW. That's how we relate with God, with Jesus, and with the Holy Spirit. That's how we enjoy our salvation in God. And that's why Christians should not be anxious about the future!

For example, you ordered pizza or lunch, or anything of value. You've saved or printed out the receipt then you wait for delivery. Pizza is coming, right? But would you get it without a proof that it was you or someone else who placed the order? No! At this point what's more important - receipt or pizza?

If you're dead hungry and become agitated and call the pizza shop and they give you assurance of delivery, how do you feel? But one thing is clear, the delivery man will not hand the pizza to you without the receipt or the order number.

Your faith is like the receipt or order number while the pizza is what you hope for.

We live by faith in God who made promises of a better future, not by the things promised in the future, for if we live by the latter, then we'd fall short of the quality and productive relationship with God, the promisor.

When the goal of your faith is to live to please God, do His biddings and continue in healthy relationship with Him, He would not just make his "acts" (physical provisions) to you but also His Way (a quality relationship with His Son, Jesus Christ), which is the surest way to get unstuck. Jesus said, "I am the way, the truth and the life...." (Jn 14:6).

> If it's not "happening now" or even "never", it doesn't always mean that you don't have faith. Your faith is not a magic wand but is dependent on God who rewards our faith with what is the best for our respective lives and purposes in due time.

Some of the generals of faith waited for some stuff which didn't happen, but they still got unstuck ultimately because they were not just expecting things to happen. They were living in the moment by faith in the reality of God's purposes for them.

I challenge you now to draw a conclusion of victory in your heart, and then, take steps of faith. *Your faith is the evidence in your hand - the receipt or order number. Hold on to it! Live with it, deliberately, purposely!*

David was motivated by God's promise of victory, held unto God for performance, drew a conclusion of victory over Goliath and took winning steps that eliminated his obstacles.

Indeed, the energy from faith can keep you through mental and physical stress.

FAITH CAN SING...

We can't possibly know and foresee all that's bound to happen in the future. That's why we must relate with God with baby-like faith.

MIMI (not real name as parents prefer anonymity) was roughly about three years old when tragedy struck. He and his friends were playing in a balcony of a storey-building. He fell from the rail and sustained head injury. About seven different surgeries were carried out on him over a short period of 18 months.

I know MIMI's parents. They're devoted believers. Anytime I saw them during this crisis, hope, faith, and confidence radiated on their faces. Though shaken, MIMI's parents' faith in the almighty God remained stronger. In the words of his mother, "If God knows about every leaf that falls to the ground; how much more, a soul created in His image. God is in charge; God knew about it and allowed it…"

The medical bills were overwhelming. His hospital room temporarily became his dad's room for about 2 months and Mom too shuttled between home and the hospital. But in the face of all of these, you can literally see faith in their eyes and candor in their countenance that MIMI's brain injury will not ultimately have much impact in his future.

It was as if the hymn "faith can sing through days of sorrow...All will be well" was written for MIMI' parents. Indeed their faith sang through the turbulence. I saw in them, faith, forgiveness, godly choice and perspectives, synergy with God in prayers and divine direction, and planning skills.

MIMI's condition is getting better, and milestones are being reached. As tough as this experience has been on his parents, they still chose to put smiles on the faces of other children by setting up a foundation to provide scholarships for children in need of school funding, among other things. Amazing!

The beauty of faith in God is that it not only works to get you unstuck but also upholds others in their difficult moments. MIMI's parents' faith works for MIMI and the results abound daily.

MIMI, his siblings and parents are still singing and will continue to sing. Amen!

I got the following testimonial from an elderly role model woman couple of weeks ago.

> *"2020-2021 has been the most difficult time of my 65+ year life. It has been extremely tough & challenging for my mental health. With the pandemic and racial injustice as a brutal backdrop, the January 6th Capitol riots & insurrection stressed my psyche to the limits. My <u>faith</u> in God and knowing He will never leave me have helped me get unstuck and given me the courage to carry on with my life, knowing that with God's love, guidance, and strength, we can overcome the hate, lies, and racism and create a better future."*

When I got that testimonial, the last stanza of the hymn, *"All Will Be Well"* written by Mary Bowley came to my mind.

"We expect a bright tomorrow;
All will be well;
Faith can sing through days of sorrow,
All, all is well.
On our Father's love relying,
Jesus every need supplying,
Or in living, or in dying,
All must be well."

Faith can sing; can hope, can wait, can assure and of course, get you unstuck!

Use your faith now! You will win!

8

PILLARS OF SUPPORT

Leveraging the Law of Synergy

"... And Saul said unto David, Go, and the LORD will be with thee."

- I Sam 17: 37

"Ye live not for yourselves; ye cannot live for yourselves; a thousand fibres connect you with your fellow-men, and along those fibres, as long sympathetic threads, run your actions as causes, and return to you as effects."

- Henry Melvill

"Synergy is what happens when one plus one equals ten or a hundred or even a thousand! It's the profound result when two or more respectful human beings determine to go beyond their preconceived ideas to meet a great challenge."

- Stephen Covey

"I truly believe in positive synergy, that your positive mindset gives you a more hopeful outlook, and belief that you can do something great means you will do something great."

- Russell Wilson

"The rate of technological and human physiological change in the 20th century has been remarkable. Beyond that, a synergy between the improved technology and physiology is more than the simple addition of the two."

- Robert Fogel

I was involved in the banks' mergers and acquisitions that took place in Nigeria when Prof. Charles Soludo was the Governor of the Central Bank of Nigeria (CBN) in 2004-2005. The CBN had rolled out a policy of compulsory recapitalization to N25 Billion for each commercial bank.

Because many of the banks were low in capital base, they had the unfortunate choice of folding out of business, recapitalize (which many of them did through Private Placement and Public Offers, and which were daunting tasks), or possibly leverage on the strength of *like-minded banks* and synergize. The latter was the preferred option. Hence the flurry of mergers and acquisitions.

There were five banks in the group for which we rendered transaction services, including a thorough due diligence by digging into their balance sheets, profit and loss accounts, contracts, and contingencies. We considered liquidity ratio, risk factors such as loan to asset portfolio, pending and likely litigations.

A key exercise in merger negotiations is the consideration of the weaknesses and strengths of the potential merging entities. This is important having regard to stock pricing, personnel and employment consideration, intellectual property, debt volumes, and a need to avoid or reduce wasting assets.

The eventual merging banks leveraged mostly on their strengths and unique selling points. They were back in banking business because, at the end of the exercise, their synergy provided the required recapitalization.

THE LAW OF SYNERGY

The law of synergy states that, *you are certain to get a lot done when you leverage on the strengths of others to supplement your areas of weakness*. You need the help of others to have the success and victory you desire. To be sure, going *solo* doesn't mean that you

131

can't get good things done, but that with synergy, you get things done easier and faster with the help of good, willing, and able like-minded people.

Collaboration, when undertaken with utmost strategy, delivers bigger and more qualitative results. Think of these terms: Amalgamation. Cooperative efforts. Collaboration. Concerted efforts. Integration. Synergy. Synthesis. United front. They explain the principle of cooperative synergy being discussed here. Certainly, two good heads are better than one!

The beauty of collaborative efforts is not only in the gregarious sociability but in the needed HELP that it offers. **No one is good enough to succeed in life without the help of others**. When you see a person, who projects the aura or image of *"I don't need anyone's help"*, or *"I know it all"*, or *"leave me alone, I know what I'm doing; I can get things done without anyone's help"*, you've seen pride in its full scale. **And fewer things in life wreck a man faster than pride**.

Proverbs 16:18 says, "Pride goes before destruction, and a haughty spirit before a fall." (NKJV). Pride is an attitude that shows that one doesn't need anyone, including God, to achieve or to get things done. God never created such a person!

> For many of us, our problems have deceived us into thinking that requesting for help from others, is a sign of weakness. Worst, many of us have been consumed by our ego such that we never come to terms with reality that we have any weakness at all.

Steven Covey described synergy as the principle of creative cooperation. According to the erudite author, "The highest forms of synergy focus on the four unique human endowments, the motive of Win/Win, and the skills of emphatic communication on the toughest challenges we face in life. What results is almost miraculous. We create new alternatives – something that wasn't there before."

Describing the principle of synergy in relative term with leadership, Covey went on: "Synergy is the essence of principle-centered leadership. It is the essence of the principle-centered parenting. It catalyzes, unifies, and unleashes the greatest powers within people. All the habits we have covered prepare us to create the miracle of synergy."

Defining synergy, Covey went further *"What is synergy? Simply defined, it means that the whole is greater than the sum of its parts. It means that the relationship which the parts have to each other is a part in and of itself. It is not a part, but the most catalytic, the most empowering, the most unifying, and the most exciting part."*

No doubt, David was a man of means. He had commanding presence, was a valiant hunter, fortune favored him, and his ancestral lineage was a plus for him. Above all, he had living and working relationship with God. Even though all these were credible credentials, David still recognized that getting over the obstacles required collaboration. But this time, he got a unique synergy – a blessing from King Saul.

> It's only the synergy where God is involved, that gets you sustainably unstuck.

SYNERGY IN INTERNAL GOVERNANCE

Synergy not only gets individuals unstuck but also corporate and governmental institutions. It is important for the different levels of government to recognize and acknowledge your weaknesses without despising your strengths – your unique selling point (USP).

To resolve internal and external national issues in some cases, conventional wisdom is engaged whereby diplomacy, intelligence and dialogues are resorted to. In other cases, however, full swing military actions are taken, especially when other viable means of conflict resolutions have been exhausted without desired results.

In resolving internal violence particularly, it's incumbent on the heads of government at various levels to collaborate with relevant stakeholders, generating ideas, delegating responsibilities to bring the administration closer to the local political components, and engaging the law of question discussed in this book. This will elicit needed materials for dialogues or provide solutions. The principle of cooperative synergy will chart the path toward getting unstuck from the impasse.

The principle of cooperative synergy in its purest sense employs participatory methodology that seeks for opinions before involvement. It's hard for one to protest what one had agreed to in the first place! Amos 3:3 asks, "Can two walk together, except they be agreed?" Certainly no!

> The platform for sustainable synergy is the ambience of conscientious agreement devoid of coercion, threat, or inducement.

Rehoboam failed to synergize with an important section of the country, and he was forever stuck! (See I Kings 12).

SYNERGY WITH ALLIES

Many local and global wars have ensued often because of the need to expand political and economic territories. The complexities that came with this led to agreements (pacts) which formed synergies among the nations concerned. But since no human words could capture all frames of minds and foresee all human eventualities, the pacts could not guarantee continued protection of the interests of parties concerned. Hence hell broke loose, and wars ensued.

During the World War II (WWII), England, United States, Soviet Union, and France were principal allies even though there were some differences among them. The purpose that united them was greater than the differences that threatened their unity. The Nazis had to be defeated. And it happened!

"In spite of these differences, the defeat of Nazi Germany was a joint endeavor that could not have been accomplished without close cooperation and shared sacrifices. Militarily, the Soviets fought valiantly and suffered staggering casualties on the Eastern Front. When Great Britain and the United States finally invaded northern France in 1944, the Allies were finally able to drain Nazi Germany of its strength on two fronts. Finally, two devastating atomic bomb attacks against Japan by the United States, coupled with the Soviets' decision to break their neutrality pact with Japan by invading Manchuria, finally led to the end of the war in the Pacific."[2]

Cooperative synergy that leverages on allies' intelligence, international diplomacy and the military institutions has been proven to be a veritable means of getting unstuck from external aggressions. However powerful a nation is, it would be difficult, if not impossible, to crush external aggressions without courting the favors of the allies with a view to consolidating their loyalties and supports.

The Nazi Germany's defeat might not have happened but for the alliances of "well-wishers." Particularly, the United States' alliance with the Soviet Union was an historic and formidable synergy. Carter Smith wrote:

"Once Germany attacked Poland in September 1939, Roosevelt worked to prepare an isolationist American public for the threat of probable U.S. involvement in the war. He helped American industry transform into "an arsenal of democracy" that produced ships, planes, and supplies faster than ever before. After Japan's attack of Pearl Harbor in 1941, he formed a close partnership with British Prime Minister Winston Churchill to lead the fight against the Axis powers."[3]

SYNERGY AND PURPOSE

You're not created to be an isolated or meandering soul. You are not an island, either. As God had said, it's not good for you to be alone. The law of synergy was first created and applied by God when He made Eve from Adam so the former could help the latter (Genesis 1:26-27; 2:21-23). God said, *"let us make man in our image..."* The "us" is the stamp of synergy from His own end!

To ordain synergy principle in our human world, God said, "... a man shall leave his father and his mother, and shall be joined to his wife; and they shall become one flesh." (Gen 1:24, AMP).

The law of synergy became more useful and wider in its application when mankind began to multiply. The growing multiplications led to increased social and spiritual issues that they had to deal with, such as problems solving, conquering kingdoms, and traversing territories. *In other words, they had to fight and win battles, not in solo efforts, but in strategic synergies.*

That's why the Bible says, "Two are better than one because they have a more satisfying return for their labor; for if either of them falls, the one will lift up his companion. But woe to him who is alone when he falls and does not have another to lift him up." (Eccl 4:9-10, AMP).

We all need some forms of mutual help at one time or the other.

THE BEST OF SYNERGIES

The best of synergies is that between you and God.

My first master's degree thesis researched on the legal and institutional frameworks for mergers and acquisitions. One of my key findings was that merger transactions could not be better than the regulatory mechanisms in a particular jurisdiction. Of course, from the cradle to the completion, the relevant law is the primary tool that provides the enabling business environment in terms of documentations, parties, structures, transactions, and timing.

Merging entities derive their relationships with one another, and with other parties outside of the merging entities from the extant law. Thus, to have seamless merger transactions, the merging entities must follow the relevant laws and regulations.

The principle of synergy in our every-day life to achieve success works the same.

> Just as in corporate mergers, the "laws of God" provide the "regulatory" ambience for successful and godly collaborations. The "law of God" is the word of God.

The synergy that will get you unshackled must be stronger than the bondage itself just as the deliverer is stronger than the oppressor. *While you might get a formidable collaboration from teaming up with people of goodwill, you can still get disappointed because the best of men are still men at their very best. It's only the synergy with God that gives absolute victory and success.*

Paul said, "…If God is on our side, who can ever be against us?" (Rom 8:31, TLB).

With God, our respective purposes are certain to happen. Amen!

SOMEBODY TO LEAN ON

We need one another!

You may be called alone but you were never created to work, live, and fight alone. This makes the law of synergy important.

There are battles that you fight alone and some that you fight corporately. Knowing the difference is a product of close relationship with the Holy Spirit. You cannot win through life alone. You need God.

> You need destiny helpers in forms of friends, marital partners, mentor(s) and "angels in human forms" – the Samaritans!

How we've all missed out in the past when we fought alone, cried alone, sorrowed alone, and got defeated alone! We thought we could get *lone victory* but got shame instead of fame, troubles instead of trophies, and setbacks instead of progress. We got failure instead of success and got defeat instead of victory because we failed to synergize with other forward-moving, like-minded, and progressive people.

The good news is that it's not too late to start again with a synergized momentum!

COMPATIBILITY THAT WORKS

Remember that there is the worst in the best of us and the best in the worst of us.

Your ability to leverage on the best of others is a wisdom in the principle of synergy. In your efforts to get unstuck, you must bear in mind that not everyone is good enough to work with you to succeed; you must identify and savor the right people, whatever it takes.

In Luke 10:1, Jesus sent out 72 disciples on a mission, two by two. Among other things, I believe Jesus had in mind the principle of synergy so that the pair could serve as support frame one to another in providing needed supplement. *However good a person is, he would need the help of others.*

FAMILY SYNERGY PRODUCES WINNING TEAMS

God deliberately designed and instituted marriage and the family unit to demonstrate the best earthly form of synergy. Of all the reasons that could probably exist for creating Eve, God chose synergy. "… but for Adam there was not found an help meet for him… And the rib, which the LORD God had taken from man, made he a woman, and brought her unto the man." (Genesis 2:20-22, KJV).

God created every family to primarily worship him, but this could not be achieved without the synergistic complements of the individuals involved. *Individuals involved in a family unit are differently endowed with unique ability for the effectuation of their God-given purposes. Good understanding of each other's different giftings and abilities, and how to productively channel them for fulfilment, is the core of the law of synergy.*

The Bible says that, "Two are better than one because they have a more satisfying return for their labor; for if either of them falls, the one will lift up his companion. But woe to him who is alone when he falls and does not have another to lift him up." (Eccl 4:9-10, AMP)

Life is ordinarily riddled with difficulties. Marital relationships could potentially compound those difficulties where there's no synergy. The probable factors that exacerbate individual differences could be spiritual, physical, psychological, or sociological. When such differences are not properly and proactively managed,

139

the intensity of the collaborative efforts becomes diffused, and conflicts become inevitable. That's why the need for synergy is super-important.

Everyone has a better part of them that could help another one in a bad situation. Lack of poor management of individual's needs and wants versus individual's inadequacies account for family violence, suicides, separations, and divorce, all of which collectively make all parties stuck in unforgiveness, assassinations, bitterness, and other related vices.

The truth is that each of the parties to failing relationships and marriages has something better to receive or give in form of supplement to produce workable relationships. *It's just that people haven't looked inward enough to generate required introspections that trigger synergistic complements.*

As a former legal advisor of a group of companies, I am aware of the accounting concept of *Balance Sheet*. It is a company's financial statement that contains its assets and liabilities. This guides the public, especially the potential investors on the prospects or otherwise of investing in it because of disclosures regarding debts, equities, assets, and liabilities.

Similarly, in family relationships, parties involved can draw out their areas of strength (assets) and weaknesses (liabilities) with a view to knowing where to leverage on and where to improve.

A practical way is for individuals in a relationship to profitably elicit their unique strength and abilities (assets) and tabulate them against their deficit habits and areas of weaknesses (liabilities). This would provide platform for what I call matching – a process where individuals in a relationship or marriage match their strength with other's weaknesses to make marital, family, or social relationships a reality. The next is to prayerfully discuss, painstakingly tolerate, and faithfully work them out.

Parents are better positioned to identify their ward's uniqueness. Then, schoolteachers, churches and community leaders would follow. The purpose is to synthesize the pieces of uniqueness to achieve results. This not only improves the families, or the organizations involved but also the societies and this invariably contributes to the realization of a better world.

The beauty of family or marriage synergy is not in the saintly individual's idiosyncratic differences but in their effective management to foster a synergy that is formidable enough to achieve success.

A successful family synergy translates to a better society because there can be no better society, city, or higher political divisions if there's no improved, disciplined individual. Every society reflects individuals "produced" by its family units.

CHURCH MINISTRY AND ADMINISTRATION SYNERGY

The body of Christ (church) is made up of persons of different abilities and callings. The wider the manifestations of these callings, the more robust the church becomes in terms of networks and operations.

While I concede that people go to churches for different purposes, most people go to church to worship God and to receive blessings from worship. The worshippers are however attracted to attend a particular local church for legitimately different reasons.

For some worshippers, the pastor's unique knowledge of the scriptures and ability to communicate effectively is a big attraction. For others, especially music lovers, it's the unique choir ministrations and choristers unique tone modulation, notes reading and voice stress, coupled with glorious performances, that attract them to church.

141

For a few others, the church unique evangelism and outreach programs are what led them to become permanent members. I have also seen where people choose to worship God in some churches because of unique emphasis on prayers.

Moreover, I have seen where believers join local churches because of the skill acquisition and vocational training programs organized by the churches in question.

Daystar Christian Center, Lagos, Nigeria is a good example. I was very privileged to have led a cell fellowship that replicated another nearby cell fellowship. The church has a wide range of skill acquisition strategies including Daystar Leadership Academy (DLA) and Daystar Skill Acquisition Program (DSAP). These avenues have brought numerous people, not just to deeper relationship with God, but also to Christ discipleship through various trainings.

Every Christian, just like anyone in the larger society, had what is called a Unique Selling Point (USP). This is an individual's unique selling abilities that potentially give him certain advantages over others. They manifest in the form of gifts, talents, skills, etc.

> Growth and multiplication in the ministry are found in a church where members' USPs are fully optimized.

The Early church probably started the idea of cell fellowship based on the principle of synergy - such that each person would impact another in a closer way.

Pastors need to leverage on the law of synergy and delegate responsibilities to capable stewards whom God has *gifted* with different abilities than the presiding pastors. For example, it's hard to conceive how a single pastor can meet the sundry needs of members on specialized areas such as finance and accounting, legal and regulatory compliance, relationship and marriage counseling, administration and leadership, logistics and transportation, guidance, and counseling, to mention a few. (See I Corinthians 12:1-31).

Before I start the next discussion, let me stress that I am not an advocate of "crowd pulling" tactics whereby a church would focus on pulling crowds to populate its local assembly just for membership or other earthly benefits.

In the context of our discussions on synergy in church administration, my emphasis is on cooperative efforts that seek to work in *stewardship*, with a view to bringing people to salvation and discipleship in Jesus Christ.

SYNERGY METAPHOR THAT REMAINS WITH US

By now, it's clear that the principle of synergy is more than a mere philosophical abstraction or sociological concept of cooperative behavior. It's God's idea that was deliberately created to guide our concerted efforts toward the fulfilment of our respective purposes in this side of eternity, individually and collectively.

Let's discuss one more insight into the law of synergy.

Genesis 7:1-3 reads:

> "And the LORD said unto Noah, come thou and all thy house into the ark; for thee have I seen righteous before me in this generation. Of every clean beast thou shalt take to thee by sevens, the male and his female: *and of beasts that are not clean by two, the male and his female*. Of fowls also of the air by sevens, the male and the female; to keep seed alive upon the face of all the earth." (Emphasis supplied).

Did you notice the uniqueness of *number two* here? Why not "one of every kind"? It cannot be! *Number one* is reserved for the Almighty God who's independently unique, with the capacity to replicate without anyone's help. Even as powerful as He was (and is), He still

143

demonstrated synergy during the creation in Genesis when he used the words, *"... Let us ..."*

> We are human beings and not designed to function or live alone without the help of others.

God designed us with imprints of pairs in our systems. These imprints are too deliberate, organized and coordinated to be accidental. Have a look at yourself. Two **eyes**. Two **ears**. Two **nostrils**. Two **hands**. Two **legs**. And a *pair of* **kidneys**!

Look at these pairs critically. How would you have been or lived if they're not in pairs? What about your **fingers** (ten) and **toes** (ten)? Why not one finger and one toe? That would be unthinkable, right?

When one gets bad, the other makes life continue. That's the essence of synergy - where you're bad, you get the good support of others!

One more thing: each of the pairs in your system enumerated above is almost of the same size, length, breadth, and height, with the other. Ordinarily, one eye should not be bigger than the other.

This tells you more about the essence of synergy - like-mindedness. **It's not enough to work in synergy; you must synergize with companions who share similar values, directions, and goals with you, or at least who're willing and ready to help you in reaching your goals.**

When you use your eyes to see or walk with your legs or wash with both hands, the metaphor of synergy is with you. When both hands wash each other, the results are better.

It's good to synergize but it's better to collaborate with like-minded fellows purposively and strategically. The similar your goals and values are, the lesser the agitations, schisms, and disagreements.

The purpose of the alliance between the United States and the Soviet Union during WWII was more important than the differences that existed between them.

United we Stand. Divided we fall!

You will win in Jesus' name!

9

BORROWED ROBE DOESN'T FIT, TAKE IT OFF!

Understanding the Law of Process

"And Saul armed David with his armor, and he put an helmet of brass upon his head; also he armed him with a coat of mail."

"And David guarded his sword upon his armor, and he assayed to go, for he had not proved it. And David said unto Saul, I cannot go with these; for I have not proved them. And David put them off him."

- I Sam 17:38-39, KJV

"He that wrestles with us strengthens our nerves and sharpens our skill. Our antagonist is our helper."

- Edmund Burke

If you're familiar with the entertainment world in America, then you must have heard of Kathie Lee Gifford. She is an embodiment of the glory that exudes from the *process of life*. She's an actress, singer, songwriter, playwright, producer, and director.

I guess you're beginning to google her name, right? Wait a minute. Kathie ran fifteen straight years' talk show, *Live with Regis and Kathie Lee (1985-2000)* which she co-hosted with Regis Philbin. She also had eleven-year show with Hoda Kotb - NBC's

TODAY *(Today with Kathie Lee and Hoda, 2008-2019).*

A charity enthusiast, Kathie, with her late husband, founded and funded charity shelters in New York for the newborn babies born with HIV and people battling crack/cocaine addiction. Today, Cassidy's Place, named after her daughter, was her brainchild. Also, Cody's House, named after her son, was the creation of Kathie and her late husband, Frank. The facility is meant to provide hope for newborn babies born with HIV and to "simply rock them – literally to love them to death", in Kathie's words.[1]

Kathie Gifford is a four-time Emmy Award Winner. When she was co-host, *Live with Regis and Kathie Lee,* she received 11 Emmy nominations. In 2015, she was inducted into the Broadcast & Cable Hall of Fame and has also been chosen to receive a star on the Hollywood Walk of Fame in 2021.[2]

But all these laurels did not just show up. And quite frankly, luck is out of it. Kathie had been through thick and thin of life and difficult experiences which she believed were part of God's processes of making her to be what she is today. She graduated from Oral Roberts University in 1975, and brimming with hope of excelling in entertainment industry, moved to Los Angeles. She'd been a born-again Christian at age eleven and was confident that, with God on her side, she would surely succeed.

But things were not as expected. She experienced interview failures and had "felt like a raw piece of meat" and suffered rejection. In her words, "I tried to convince myself it was all part of the learning process and that I would get better with each audition." Her optimism and patience paid her after all; she got a dream job. "…the legendary producer Ralph Edwards walked over to me to shake my hand." … "Welcome to Ralph Edwards productions." He smiled graciously. "Welcome to *Name That Tune."*

Past failures and rejections can be fertile grounds for greatness if you can connect the underlying dots successfully. This is true of Kathie Gifford. According to her, "...I learned two hundred songs in five days and shot the shows for the entire years in a few weeks." And here's the thrilling experience that makes one forget the agonies of the *process time.* "We taped at the NBC studios in Burbank right next to *The Tonight Show,* and finally, I thought, *So this is what it's like to make a living doing what you love to do...*", She said.

I believe Kathie Gifford could resonate with David when he saw the giant Goliath going down in agony. Her experience was similar. "A few weeks later we wrapped the season, and I headed to the car in the parking lot feeling elated. It had gone well. I hadn't made one mistake in two hundred songs..."[4] Awesome!

I guess David too had that feeling: *"Yeah! Goliath is on the floor; the fiery stone has eaten deep into his eye. My sling had made no mistake. Goliath went down for it just as lions and bears could not escape its fiery darts..."*

That's what happens when past experiences prepare you for victory!

Bravo David! Kudos to Kathie Lee Gifford!!

> The secrets of people are masked with the obscuring covers of history. It's the searchlight of truth, diligence and dints of hard work that illuminate them.

We all agree that there are lots of successful people who went through high and low periods of life before they rose to the Olympian heights of fortune, even though their silent travails might have gone unsung. But I guess what many people do not know or at least, talk about are the *silent dots* that connect the struggling and the success times.

These *silent dots* are spelt *process* and shall be the focus of this chapter.

THE LAW PROCESS

The law of process states that *everything of value is a function of series of underlying processes that ultimately attract their equivalent success and victory*. Permitting some exceptions, it's the sum of your life's *historical processes* that gives us the value of your current life.

In financial terms, the current fair market value (FMV) of a property is generally determined by its historical cost (base). Thus, your *base* is your process!

If you want to invest in real estate, you'd consider many factors including the land itself, the surrounding, foundation, builder's integrity, quality, and quantity of materials used, and some procurement documentations and activities.

A right-minded person would not consult an infant who claims to be a consultant cardiologist because he had not passed through a process of learning and experience.

If you want to know why you are stuck, then think about your *historical processes*.

THE REJECTED WEAPONS

David rejected Saul's armor because he had not tested, proven, or trained with it – he was not used to it.

In the events that preceded David's fight with Goliath, we read how King Saul offered his armor to David and how David rejected this "golden" help. It was more than a mere offer; Saul actually "armed

David with his armor" and "put a helmet of brass upon" David's head. Besides, Saul also "armed him with a coat of mail."

To be clear, historically, "coat of mail" means a special protective armor coat that's made of overlapping metal rings or plates.

Ordinarily this type of "special favor" by Saul is not what should be rejected. The following historical facts about mail armor will interest you.

> It "… provided an effective defense against slashing blows by edged weapons and some forms of penetration by many thrusting and piercing weapons; in fact, a study conducted at the Royal Armouries at Leeds concluded that «it is almost impossible to penetrate using any conventional medieval weapon»… Generally speaking, mail's resistance to weapons is determined by four factors: linkage type (riveted, butted, or welded), material used (iron versus bronze or steel), weave density (a tighter weave needs a thinner weapon to surpass), and ring thickness (generally ranging from 18 to 14 gauge (1.02–1.63 mm diameter) wire in most examples). Mail, if a warrior could afford it, provided a significant advantage when combined with competent fighting techniques."[5]

Why would David then reject such a great favor? I want to believe that David placed God above all persons and things and had unflinching confidence in *God's dealings with him* including God' process of forming him to be who he was at the point of his encounter with Goliath.

He had said, "Praise the LORD, my protector! He trains me for battle and prepares me for war." (Ps 144:1, GNT). The word "prepares" means "trains", "teaches" all connote a process through which one understands, masters and can competently use or defend a thing. *Preparation* and *process* go together.

Have you proved your weapon?

The Hebrew word for the word *"prove"* is to test or try. It is in that context that David rejected Saul's' armor reasoning that he had not *proved (tested or tried)* it. (See I Samuel 17:39). To prove a thing or test an instrument is to try its efficacy.

The law of process motivates you to sharpen your skills, go back to school, learn new skills, and improve your networks to gain new contacts. It is often said that it is insanity to do things repeatedly and expect a different result. You must test potential methodologies and plans of action which metaphorically, could be potential weapon in your arsenal.

Your safety and eventual victory do not depend on the size of your weaponry. Psalm 33:16 says, 'The king is not saved by the great size of his army; A warrior is not rescued by his great strength." (AMP). Besides, "The horse is prepared for the day of battle, but the victory belongs to the LORD." Prov 21:23 (NLT).

Your weapon could be good temperament, character, integrity, honesty, and good attitude. The victory, success, healing, and the solutions that you desire are masked in the accumulated daily experiences of the past and present years. That is what we see in David who developed warfare and battle skills from his past daily experiences with God, the Commander of the Captains of the host of heaven.

IDENTIFY YOUR ACHILLES HEEL

Have you ever heard of Achilles heel? Achilles, according to Greek mythology, was foretold to die young. To prevent this misfortune, his mother went to dip him into a magical river to fortify him and make him invulnerable. Doing this, his mother held him by heel thereby making the heel unfortified. Achilles grew and became a great fighter. He was shot with poisonous arrow at the unfortified point of his heel. It then became a metaphorical expression to describe a person's week and vulnerable area as his Achilles heel.

Have you identified your Achilles heel and dealt with it? When you confront the battles against afflictions of your life with untested kits and unproven armor, or a borrowed robe, you are at the risk of dangers because a borrowed robe would either be too tight or too loose. When it is too tight, you become uncomfortable and imbalanced for the battle ahead.

When your kit is too loose, you get exposed because you have some areas of your body uncovered and become vulnerable to the attacks of the enemies.

> You need balance and stamina to get unstuck. But you don't get these in another person's robe. All you get is distraction that comes from constant adjustments of armors that you're not used to.

THE PRINCIPLES OF THE LAW OF PROCESS

Let's consider the principles of the law of process and their nuances.

1. PROCESS SHOWS YOUR REAL SELF

The sum of your experiences in life, from cradle to old age, is wrapped up in phenomenon called the *process of life*. During this process, you'd have a random or calculated discovery of your identity. Every difficult experience introduces you to yourself, exposes your strength and weaknesses. And so, life's difficult experiences should make you *look inward*, keep focus, *"discover yourself"* and discover ways of improving yourself to meet up with demands of your purpose in life.

David had similar experiences and sometimes failed but leaned from them. *In most cases, our problems are not really our past bad times (which should not be excuses for failures) but that we failed to bring up good lessons from the experiences of past dirty days.*

As in the case of David's adulterous affairs with Bathsheba, your process time reveals your limitations, weaknesses, and vulnerabilities. (see II Samuel 11). That's a good time to discover that you're not complete in yourself without God's help.

2. PROCESS PROVES YOU

In the process of time, David had animals, rodents, and insects as neighbors while fleeing from King Saul's arrows. Some ridiculed him and labelled him as a renegade. He even had to pretend to be insane at some point to escape being lynched. The pains he suffered, the shame he faced, and the burden he bore toughened him and built resilience in him and made him more determined. These were some of his connecting dots to his eventual exalted position of a king.

The process of time tests you to know the specimen you're made of.

The truth is, killing bear and lions with bare hands were necessary experiences for David to slay the giant Goliath. *Bear and lions are dangerous carnivorous animals that are difficult to be killed with bare hands without certain fighting skills.* Your process time toughens you and sharpens your skills. I agree with Edmund Burke who says, *"He that wrestles with us strengthens our nerves and sharpens our skill. Our antagonist is our helper."*

3. PROCESS DEVELOPS YOUR WAITING CAPACITY

Patience is a rare but needed virtue to get you ahead.

We live in the world today that honors "patience" in the dictionary rather than in its possession.

> Patience is not waiting idly expecting sudden good happenings; it's keeping godly attitude and keeping hope alive while waiting.

Waiting patiently does not mean doing nothing; it means doing things expectantly, differently. While waiting, you reflect, perspire, strategize, and sometimes question some of your actions that led to your current situation. While waiting, don't stop praying or stop reading and meditating on the word of God. In short, you are active but probably not on what you were doing before.

Afflictions are not forever. Every problem has a *shelf life*. This realization will help you to keep hope alive as you wait patiently for the propitious time because God has already set time for each event of life. (Ecclesiastes 3:1,11). David realized this and said that he waited "patiently and expectantly for the LORD…". (Ps 40:1-2, AMP). His waiting experience *proved* him during failures and dangers till what God foretold came to pass – he became a King!

King Saul could not wait for prophet Samuel who had commanded him to wait and offered sacrifice which was meant to be offered by a priest. This later cost him his royalty (I Samuel 13:8-14).

James 1:4 says, "And let endurance have its perfect result *and* do a thorough work, so that you may be perfect and completely developed [in your faith], lacking in nothing." (AMP). However distasteful your experiences of the moment might be, don't lose your patience. Focus on the victory ahead and be motivated by it.

When you rush to do what's not ripe for action, you just put yourself in the class of the lazy people because impatience and laziness have the same reward – regrets! Proverbs 16:32 cautions us: "Better a patient person than a warrior, one with self-control than one who takes a city." (NIV).

The good news is that your success and victory are worth the waiting!

4. PROCESS MATURES YOU

Maturity is where the growth is.
No one achieves greatness without growth.
At the core of the law of process is the "miracle" of maturity.

You've probably missed out on some opportunities for success and victory not because of lack of fortune but because of paucity of emotional and intellectual capacities to handle them - to adapt, contain, or otherwise *live life forward*. Whichever way you look at it, capacities are products of inspirations, perspirations, and experiences, all of which work with maturity.

Romans 5:3-5 says, "… let us exult in our sufferings *and* rejoice in our hardships, knowing that hardship (distress, pressure, trouble) produces patient endurance; and endurance, proven character (spiritual maturity); and proven character, hope *and* confident assurance [of eternal salvation] …" (AMP).

> Life is charitable enough to give all of us experiences but stingy enough to hide from us how to use them in a particular way.

You develop capacities to handle life affairs, including success or failures during your process time. You also learn maturity which helps you to maximize experiences to get returns of victories, success, achievements, and greatness that you desire. Endure discipline and come out with results and not excuses. Remember, excuses regretfully remain barren.

God's kingdom resources are committed to those who are matured. *Among other things, maturity is the art of forming judgment to take productive God-glorifying decisions at crucial times. Both the experiences leading to forming judgment and post-judgment experiences are necessary factors to crystalize you into your God-given dream future.*

MATURITY PREPARES YOU FOR BETTER CHOICES

Maturity prepares you for important choices like marriage, businesses, career path, financing and refinancing, your health and your kids' welfare. *Maturity is thus an important product of experience, the core of the law of process.*

For example, you need maturity to handle finances otherwise you'll be stuck in debts. The more you grow, the larger your capacity to absorb tough experiences without being broken. You then have increased ability to successfully manage and lead when opportunities come.

It's hard if not impossible to do nothing worthwhile with what you have and then expect someone to hire you for leadership role. It is when you do something with what you have that you acquire cognate experiences that unfold management capacity.

Start doing something worthwhile and never be satisfied with the status quo and mediocrity. Develop maturity by converting your experiences to worthwhile ventures. The more you utilize your experiences productively, the more matured you become, and this is a sure way to attract blessings, profitable relationships, and opportunities for greatness.

5. PROCESS GROWS YOUR FAITH CAPACITY

Faith in God is developed in the process of discomfort and challenges.

After God had liberated the Israelites from Egypt, He did not let them pass through a shorter route which was Philistines' territory, knowing that they would face wars and retreat to Egypt. (See Exodus 13:17). It would have been the Israelites' delight to avoid walking stressful, energy-sapping, and tortuous paths to get to the promise land. No one wants stress. But God's process for them was far better than what they would have wanted.

That generation of Israelites was a group of highly vulnerable, mostly harmless, people who were naïve to meet up with the articulate veterans of the Philistines. They probably had lost their fighting skills to prolonged decades of domestication and servitude with hard labor in Egypt. So, they needed to develop crucial skills and growth that could be garnered in the process of maturity that God subjected them to.

> The glory of growing through adversities is not in making masochists of us but the stable and sustainable virtues that stem from a proven character. It is not that God lacks feelings but that He places our development of godly character and values above meaningless comfort and indulgence. He knows that the character that we fail to build would eventually destroy the empires we build!

God gave the Israelites the *process experience* to mature their relationship with Him, by expecting them to live by faith and to overcome dangers of men and beasts. By driving out the enemies away little by little, he was expecting them to develop their spiritual muscle-powers as well as faith usage in total dependence on Him for victory "until they have increased enough to take possession of the land." (Exd 23:30, NIV)

What you withstood and resisted during your *process periods* can no longer terrorize you because you've grown and developed some resistance. And, as we discussed under the law of choice, *motion and resistance go together.* The resistance builds confidence, candor, and capacity all of which are comebacks from hard times.

Like Paul, when you have the confidence that you "...can do all things through Christ who strengthens" you, what else can life threaten you with? When the process of growth has toughened you to a near-death experience, again like Paul, and you see death as personal gain, what else can death threaten you with?

Your initial setbacks aren't conclusions of your failures. It only means that you're probably not getting some stuff done in a right way. Figure out what is missing, and if you are unable to do this, then, consult the right person.

DON'T BE INFLEXIBLE

In Mark 2:21-22 Jesus says, "No one sews a patch of unshrunk (new) cloth on an old garment; otherwise the patch pulls away from it, the new from the old, and the tear becomes worse. No one puts new wine into old wineskins; otherwise the [fermenting] wine will [expand and] burst the skins, and the wine is lost as well as the wineskins. But new wine must be put into new wineskin." (AMP).

What does that mean? Changes, developments, growth, improvements are all products of *a process* during when God expects us to change old habits and old ways of doing things that sap our creative energies and get us stuck in old ways of living.

God's great ideas, revelations, and new improved ways of doing things to get better results are hanging unutilized because the old wine skins (our unregenerate minds and countenances) would break in the absence of a maturity process.

The following are possible flexible ways you can adapt while in process of maturity.

1. Right equipment is important: Since the law of process touches on improvements, trainings, testing, it's important to get the equipment right, from the outset. In this context, equipment refers to the combination of tools, device, or any useful materials in "chiseling and crafting" you into the person that attracts the type of victory or success meant for you.

The useful tools vary according to what is to be achieved and the areas of endeavor. For example, for attorneys, media men, pastors, or public speakers, a good tool of trade is a mastery of the language of the jurisdiction. Master the language *registers* of your field. The Bible says, "if the axe is dull more strength is needed." (Eccl 10:10). Your axe connotes your equipment.

Old wine skins could be old technology - old way of doing things. You have always heard of the saying, "don't reinvent the wheel." I know it's an adage. That's fine. If the wheel is useful then all you do is improve on it. But what happens if the "wheel" is so bad that it can't be improved upon to achieve new and progressive results?

> Whether to improve on the wheel or reinvent it, I think what matters to you is to move the wheel to get you to your purpose. The most important thing is to savor and embrace new technologies and adapt them to suit what you want to get done.

2. Get the strategy right: Strategy is a military term that encompasses the mechanism of mobilizing and directing the operation of the military in war time. It connotes operational tactics including secrets and modalities. Strategy is a blueprint of your actions, technically called the drawing board to which you can always turn in the events of unforeseen circumstances.

Strategies include duration, quantities, personnel (who's doing what), government relations and compliance mechanisms, organogram, contingencies (plans A, B, C, etc.) and importantly, appropriate technology.

To get unstuck in life, strategies are *sine qua non* and must not be inflexible.

3. Regularly maintain your body: Your spirit is vital to your success and so is your soul. But as important as your spirit and soul are, they can't be substituted for your healthy body.

The cells in your body make you a living being. These cells must be renewed continually by reproducing themselves and dying to keep you healthy. How these cells will cooperate with you to live well to fulfill your dreams depends on a lot of factors including your commitment to eating balanced diets, regular exercise, good sleep, regular medical checkups, and keeping a sound mind and good spirit.

Your physical body and its component parts are important to the fulfilment of your purpose.

4. Change what's not working: Changing the old wineskins means changing what's not working. Staying stuck with old and unprofitable methods can have disastrous consequences. You may need to embrace a change of technology, change of personnel, change of (physical and human) environments, or change of duration. This is important to *create room for what is new in terms of momentum, quality, capacity, and value.*

In Genesis 26:16-22, Isaac was not unstuck until there was change in his physical environment, at least twice. Most people want progress but fear changes. Many people destined to become "butterflies" in their multi-color regalia are stuck as "larva" because they have refused to embrace the changes required for their transformation.

Changing old wineskins sometimes include improving on what's performing below capacity. Life is designed to release your blessings after certain changes have been made, including changes to your body, desires, tastes, friendships, relationship, tools, and of course, your environment.

5. Excel on what's working: Success is never final. Success becomes sustainable when it reproduces. There've been many former successful people just as we've seen once successful business ventures that are now bankrupt.

A key to staying successful is to multiply your success. This is achieved by creating succession plan.

DON'T BREAK DURING THE PROCESS

The world biggest cruise ship - Harmony of the Seas (*Harmony*) – is notable for redefining cruise ships and vacations by many standards. Standing at an imposing height of 155.6 ft and length of 1,188 ft, *Harmony* has the capacity to accommodate about 6000 passengers on board, with VIP lounge, shopping center, and a host of amenities of a modern urbanized community.

Five times bigger than the *Titanic, Harmony's* magnificent 18 stories are manned by 2,300 crew members across 72 nationalities of the world. If you're a lover of wine and drinks, you'll have the pleasure of having your wine mixed and served by robots.

The seagoing five-star hotel cruise ship was completed in 2015.

But this incredible masterpiece was not made overnight. It took about three years to build and that reflects on its cost - a whooping cost of $1.35 Billion as at 2015. While under construction, over three thousand workers and different professionals were on site working assiduously 24/7.

161

Welders, carpenters, engineers, and a host of technicians were hitting, bending, paneling, and beating this great structure from many sides. Errors, corrections, adjustments, reconstructions were inevitable.

As I can imagine, if *Harmony* were able to speak, it would have shouted, *"hey, what the heck is going on? What exactly do you want to make out of me that you have humiliated, mutilated, and pierced me this way?*

I can also guess the engineers and workers would have responded: *"Oh no, sorry about your pain. When we're done, you'll be the best of your type in the world. You're probably having all these torture and pains because you'll soon become what none of the earlier ships ever became. Keep enduring. 2015 would soon be here..."*

The point I'm making is that, the glory that comes with your future is worth the training that comes with the process of life. Your past experiences are as good as weapons to fight and win the victory that you desire when you rightly connect the dots.

You aren't going to have everything you want during training because your choices would be limited. That's why it's called *training*.

I was in a conversation recently with a military man scheduled to begin training in few days. As characteristic of me, I started teasing him, making pseudo salutations, and mumbling incoherent orders. Then we burst out laughing. I said to him, "now you're going to enjoy and have fun during your training, aren't you?"

He gave me a wry look, supposing that I came from the moon. "Did you say there's fun in this training I'm talking about? If you have fun in this type of training then there's a problem...", he responded. And, nodding in approval, I said, "...got you; you're now talking to me."

Your past is now your history over which you have no control except to change its effect in your life. One of the ways to do this is by your choices on friendships and relationships, time, career, and environment, all of which mold your character. *Thus, midwifed by the process of time, your character is a child of your history and your choices. You must therefore, as part of your growing process in daily living, be flexible to embrace changes that can crystalize you into the person that God intended for you.*

When you're flexible enough to let the process of time build godly character in you, success or victory then becomes predictable because God would be pleased with you, and you'll enjoy men's goodwill.

You do not grow and get used to an armor overnight. *You grow into maturity by diligent studying and learning – learning from experiences, from books, and from others.* Learning involves failing many times and learning from mistakes and failures. What comes out of those experiences is, among other things, *"familiarization with your weapons"* to know their efficacies, when and how to use them.

When you approach every problem that comes up against you with a positive posture of a learning pupil, with desire to improve and become a better version of yourself, your sense of maturity will certainly reward you. Keep learning from each experience and don't be weary of this practice for this moves you in the direction of victory.

Don't expect to be perfect for no one in history ever achieved greatness through subjective sense of perfection but by dints of hard work, determination, learning from mistakes and courting improvements like a beautiful fiancée. Practice does not make perfection, for if it were, all the lackluster and lazy attempts would have suddenly transformed the most vicious of all persons into a saintly angel! Practice makes improvements! Success is a golden item made up of many broken materials that are improved upon by a tenacious goldsmith!

Consider all your experiences as means to an end – a training that's necessary for the type of success and victory desired.

Like David, learn how to use the process of life to get you unshackled.

10
CHOOSING FIVE SMOOTH STONES

Engaging the Law of Craft

"And David put them off him. And he took his staff in his hand, and chose him five smooth stones out of the brook, and put them in a shepherd's bag which he had, even in a scrip; and his sling was in his hand: and he drew near to the Philistine."

- I Sam 17:40, KJV

"Without craftsmanship, inspiration is a mere reed shaken in the wind".

- Johannes Brahms

"It is possible to fly without motors, but not without knowledge and skill."

- Wilbur Wright

"Your skill can be either an asset or a liability."

-Justin Ho

"A winner is someone who recognizes his God-given talents, works his tail off to develop them into skills, and uses these skills to accomplish his goals."

- Larry Bird

I received the piece of writing in the next paragraph from a couple while writing this book. They have been role models and have used the law of craft to bless many people across various cultural and racial backgrounds.

*"Having worked extremely hard for most of our lives to master our engineering **craft**, we've learned to count our blessings from God and appreciate all the educational, training, and work opportunities that have been available to us. To ensure that others (who may not have the monetary resources to pursue an engineering degree) can achieve their potential, we have established scholarships at our alma mater to pay for their university education."*

THE LAW OF CRAFT

The law of craft states that ***the art that is masterfully perfected in craftmanship, technique, and usage, makes margin of success predictable; an improved skill creates an expanded skillset.*** Your improved skill and expanded skillset in a particular discipline invariably predict the value that is placed on you.

The principles of the law of craft amplify the essentials of skill, especially the problem-solving and wisdom-embellished skills that break barriers. Remember that wisdom is the right application of your knowledge.

THE GOD OF CRAFT IN HUMAN BODY

God is full of skill, craft, and ingenuity.

You do not have to look far or search deep to see God's skills in display. Just look up, look down, and above all, look at yourself.

Take a reflection on each organ in your body. Though there's no universally scientifically agreed number, it has been established that human body has over *seventy-nine organs*, with different organic frames including muscular, digestive, respiratory, urinary, reproductive, endocrine, circulatory, and nervous.[1]

According to a recent research, you are made up of an estimated *thirty trillion cells* in your body and having two hundred types of cells different in weight and sizes. An average body makes about two to three million red blood cells every second. Put it another way, about a hundred and seventy-three to two hundred and fifty-nine billion red blood cells are made per day in an average human body. The cells die and are replaced simultaneously.[2]

All of these accentuate the marvelous wisdom of God in making you. No wonder the Psalmist says, "Thank you for making me so wonderfully complex! It is amazing to think about. Your workmanship is marvelous—and how well I know it. (Ps 139:14, TLB). The least you could do is to acknowledge and draw inspirations from the creative ingenuity of the almighty God.

THE GOD OF CRAFT IN THE PHYSICAL WORLD

The magnificence of this physical world overwhelmingly displays the unmatched creative competence of God. During Job's ordeals, he frantically made sundry but vain efforts in unraveling the unquestionable status of God regarding His person, His creations, and His ways. Elihu, one of his friends counselled him, "Certainly, God is so great that he is beyond our understanding. The number of his years cannot be counted. (Job 36:26, GW). Elihu continued:

> "He draws up the drops of water,
> which distill as rain to the streams;
> the clouds pour down their moisture
> and abundant showers fall on mankind.
> Who can understand how he spreads out the clouds,
> how he thunders from his pavilion?
> See how he scatters his lightning about him,
> bathing the depths of the sea.
> This is the way he governs the nations
> and provides food in abundance.
> He fills his hands with lightning
> and commands it to strike its mark. (Job 36:27-32, NIV).

You may read Job chapters 37 and 38 for further understanding of God's magnificent creative abilities.

Think about the celestial bodies, the sun, moon, stars in their constellation, the galaxy, and the milky-way.[3] Consider the terrestrial world. "Terrestrial planets have a solid planetary surface, making them substantially different from the larger gaseous planets, which are composed mostly of some combination of hydrogen, helium, and water existing in various physical states."[4] That's why the Bible says, "The LORD created the earth by his wisdom..." (Prov 3:19, GNT).

The solar system consists of traditional nine planets, but scientists have discovered the tenth - ("Planet X").[5]

> ## As God's creature, you're a beneficiary of His creativity, wisdom, and craftsmanship. This is the amazing realization that David had in his relationship with God.

DAVID'S FIGHTING SKILLS

In the last chapter we talked about David putting off King Saul's unproven armor. What is then David's proven armor? Anointed crafts! He deployed the law of craft under the inspiration of the Almighty God.

David's manipulation of the stones and his sling is no ordinary feat. It represents skills woven in grace and grace manifesting in craft. Hence the sobriquet, "... Saul has slain his thousands, and David his tens of thousands." (I Sam 18:7). Little wonder that he once said, "Praise the LORD, my protector! He trains me for battle and prepares me for war." (Ps 144:1, GNT).

Every genuine child of God is in a greater advantage when it comes to richness of the winning skills because, "God has hidden all the treasures of wisdom and knowledge in Christ." (Col 2:3, GW). God's wisdom is seen virtually in all His creations – visible and invisible. (See Romans 1:20).

THE FIVE SMOOTH STONES

The narrative of David's fight with Goliath is silent on whether David worked on the stones at all. The storyline appears to indicate that David went straight to the brook and hand-picked ready-to-use five smooth stones and put them in his bag. The accustomed ease with which David acted as captured in the narrative smacks of David routine exercise. (See I Samuel 17:40).

Hunting with sling and smooth stones were part of the traditional weaponry in those days. For example, Judges 20:16 says, "Among all this people there were seven hundred chosen men lefthanded; every one could sling stones at an hair breadth, and not miss." (See also I Chron 12:2; II Chron 26:14).

As important as your raw talents, giftings and potentials are, they are not enough to take you to stardom. You must cultivate those potentials in the line of your chosen vocation by improving on them. You need education, trainings, and other means to strengthen your skills even as you continue to seek intimacy with God.

> The more you educate your ignorance and seek intimacy with God of wisdom, the sharper your skills and the better you are as a person. The more you read, study, and seek knowledge, the more you educate your ignorance and grow.

Working with proven and familiar skills is wisdom but fighting with untested armor is insanity. *A masterful blend of tested principles is an effective workmanship in fighting and winning cycles of afflictions.*

The more David walked and worked with God, the wider and stronger his skillset became as he drew inspiration from God on how to fight the battles of life. This is David speaking:

> ·"The Lord himself is my inheritance, my prize. ... He guards all that is mine. He sees that I am given pleasant brooks and meadows as my share! What a wonderful inheritance! I will bless the Lord who counsels me; he gives me wisdom in the night. He tells me what to do. (Ps 16:5-7, TLB).

PRINCIPLES OF THE LAW OF CRAFT

Let us discuss some proven principles of the law of craft.

1. Improve your skills

Improving your skills is a sure way to prepare for the future.

David's five smooth stones were in ready-to-use form in his bag on the day he killed Goliath. Success is not a day's job. It's in the combination of little right steps taken at different times in the process of time.

Avoid fire-brigade-approach to problem-solving. Success is predictable. Prepare. Work on yourself. Improve. Improvise. Sharpen your skill.

The sixteenth American President, Abraham Lincoln said, "I will study and prepare myself, and someday my chance will come." That's the winning attitude you should keep.

Demosthenes (384 - 322 BCE) of the 4th century, the greatest orator of the ancient time, did not start as a genius. In fact, he was laughed off the rostrum at his first public speech. But with self-improvement and skillset expansion, he overcame his speech defects. To overcome stammering and difficulty calling out some letters, he practiced by standing at the shore with pebbles in his mouth.

One of Demosthenes' major chores was practicing speaking in front of a large mirror. With disciplined program, he overcame "his weaknesses and improved his delivery, including diction, voice, and gestures. According to one story, when he was asked to name the three most important elements in oratory, he replied "Delivery, delivery and delivery!"[6]

Demosthenes later thrived in his speech writing, legal and political careers and became one of the greatest orators in ancient Greece.

2. Widen your skillset

Your skillset is your range of special abilities or competencies required to do your job. *If you are a salesperson, your necessary skillset would be good manners, good interpersonal relationship, networking, and friendship, planning and time management. For a manager, important skillsets include a team spirit (replacing I, Me, and Mine with We, Us and Ours), human relations, time management, project management and effective reporting standards.*

Whatever it is that you've got to do to move forward productively, do it excellently such that you have a branding of excellence in that area.

Develop the character for being civil, respectful, and detail oriented.

Cultivate the habit of going the extra mile (within reasonable limits of godly character) to satisfy those who are at the receiving end of your services such as clients, customers, managers, bosses, and dependents.

The more satisfied your clients and customers, the more they can count on you for future services. Let your services improve humanity and glorify God. This earns you a large volume of referrals with high possibility of expanding your clientele base. This is when excellence becomes light. The people will see your light and give glory to God. (See Matthew 5:16; Philippians 2:15).

Like money, excellence naturally attracts value and value drivers, including market leaders, captains of industry and even people in authority. *The unfolding of your excellent skills is a doorway to greatness.* That's why the Bible says, "Do you see a man skillful *and* experienced in his work? He will stand [in honor] before kings; He will not stand before obscure men." (Prov 22:29, AMP).

- "who excels in his work" (NKJV)
- "who is skilled in their work" (NIV)
- "truly competent workers" (NLT)
- "efficient in his work" (GW)

In most cases, wider skillset goes with competence and excellence. The more you improve your skills the more competent and excellent you are, and besides good character, very few things take you to stardom than excellence. In fact, excellence is inseparably part of good character!

Edmund Hillary improved his climbing skillset after failing at first attempt. His next attempt in 1953 took him to the top of the world, literally.

David the beast killer became the giant killer. Thanks to his expanded skillset.

This leads us to the next principle in the law of craft, training.

3. Effective training and development

Since no one was born with most, if not, all the required skillsets for excellence, it thus behooves you to cultivate the habit of a diligent student by giving yourself to learning, training, studying and never stop improving yourself.

You must savor training and developmental programs. Effective training programs boost performance and increase outputs. The Bible says, "If the ax is dull and its edge unsharpened, more strength is needed, but skill will bring success." (Eccl 10:10, NIV).

Ax connotes tools and sharpening symbolizes training. As cutting tools perform better upon sharpening so is effective personnel training; it yields maximum performance. I want to believe that God had training and development in mind, when the Bible says, "As iron sharpens iron, so one man sharpens [and influences] another [through discussion]." (Prov 27:17, AMP).

A man is a combination of his face, visage, thoughts, physique, and spirit, all of which often find expression in his countenance.

> The excellence that gets you unstuck would come from what you do daily to improve yourself and the skill that will bring you success is the one you improve!

SHARPEN YOUR COUNTENANCE

First, you are not an island and so you can't possibly know or have everything to succeed without the help of others. Second, knowledge, by its very nature, is relative and bound to be outdated when it's not updated. That's why all accredited professional bodies require their members to undergo trainings as often as possible.

Most organizations have in-service trainings for their staff. If you head an organization or a corporation, it is very imperative that you include a substantial funding for training and development in your budget each financial year.

Few years into my law practice experience, I was neck-deep in corporate commercial and energy law practice as our clientele base widened locally and internationally at the law office where I worked at that time. We started receiving briefs globally on legal aspects of cross-border investments and repatriation of foreign proceeds, especially the tax aspect. The local companies too wanted to know how the growing trends in local and international taxations would impact their business and dividends distributions. Thanks to our visionary partners and the Managing Partner who were quick to enroll us in a training program to be better suited to meet the needs of our clients.

Shortly, my direct supervisor and I became a chartered tax advisors. This experience was about two years after completing my first graduate program (thesis-tracked) with my dissertation on the *Legal and Institutional Frameworks for Mergers and Acquisition*. The focus of my research increased my value in the law office.

Our new improved skillset resulted in a win-win business relationship with our clients. Our capacity was strengthened, our client-base broadened and their needs were met and exceeded. With this additional expertise we could offer, we got many referrals; many with whom the office has maintained a retainer till date. As we increased in competence and capacity which resulted in the increase of our clientele, hiring more attorneys became inevitable.

As humans, we are designed to be flexible and improve. Consider when a baby is born and how he grows from the cradle to adulthood. Training (growing) is the bridge that links the childhood to adulthood. That's why Proverbs 22:6 says, "Train up a child in the way he should go [teaching him to seek God's wisdom and will for his abilities and talents], Even when he is old he will not depart from it." (AMP).

Apostle Paul said, "When I was a child, I talked like a child, I thought like a child, I reasoned like a child; when I became a man, I did away with childish things." (I Cor 13:11, AMP). That's a product of training and improvements.

> With a perpetual commitment to training, your mind becomes flexible and flexible minds (with sound judgment) appeal to greater advantage in relationship and business building.

Many years later after leaving that law firm I told you about, I started my own private practice. I saw the need to improve my skill, so I registered for a graduate program in 2014 and graduated from the University of Houston Law Center in 2015, with an *LL.M.* in Tax Law.

About three years later, I felt an increased need to update my knowledge on legal contracts drafting, review and negotiations. So, I became a member of the Association of International Petroleum Negotiators (AIPN).

Knowledge not updated will soon be outdated!

4. Right personnel in right positions

Whether as a person or a business, your best assets are your best people. They may be friends or business associates or staff. Savor their best interest because if you do, with their cooperation you will find it easier to realize goals.

According to Zig Ziglar, "The great managers from all fields know that when they put people first, their effectiveness and efficiency improve". Zoltan Merszel, who left Dow Chemical to become president of Occidental Petroleum, said, "My philosophy is that people make business; technology is a distant second."[7]

You must maintain effective human resources and ensure that certain policies and programs are in place to boost workers morale, to reward exceptional performances and to punish or deter anti-progress elements.

You must never make a mistake of deploying untested and unreliable toolkits. Nothing disappoints like working with unproven equipment or unreliable personnel. It's like striking a pledge with an unreliable person in trouble time. The Bible says, "putting confidence in an unreliable person in times of trouble is like chewing with a broken tooth or walking on a lame foot." (Prov 25:19, NLT).

5. Right equipment and technologies

Part of training to succeed is the choice of right tools, right personnel, and the required trainings. A good mastery of the law of craft is reflected in your ability to say or demonstrate a "NO" to wrong tools usage, unapologetically and emphatically. David said "NO" to King Saul's armor intelligently. "…David told Saul. "I've never had any practice doing this." (I Sam 17:39, GW).

Expand your toolkits and sort out the ones that deliver the maximum results. This is the process of matching. Remember to put round pegs in round holes. It's a waste of energy, time, and resources to use wrong tools on a project in which you've invested a lot of resources. The result is like someone promising you what he does not have - an empty promise.

Using wrong tools maximizes ineffectiveness and delivers woeful results. It's not worth it!

SKILL ALONE IS NOT ENOUGH

Your skill alone is not the sole factor for success.

We have seen many soccer or football teams with highly skilled players lose their games. A lot of highly skilled people are behind bars and many more walk freely on the roads who prefer to end their lives in suicide. So many soldiers with the best of fighting skills have perished at warfronts.

We have seen many gifted people who perished in poverty just as innumerable company of wise people have been victims of ignominy and shamefully barred from the presence of the nobles. To be clear, in pursuit of success, skill alone is not enough; neither is gifting. A godly character is a bedrock of sustainable success.

It is no use having improved skills and expanded levels of capacities when we lack the moral fiber of character to contain the attendant responsibilities or sustain the ensuing success. A man of great skills and excelling trajectory who is bereft of integrity is pretty much like a skyscraper with a weak foundation. He will collapse under pressure in a matter of time!

Fame, prosperity, victories, and mostly all worthwhile achievements often come with attendant pressures that conspicuously put a capital question mark on your success. It's the strength of your character that upholds them like supporting frames of a house.

I remember an old story of a Boat builder (Builder) and his apprentice. The Builder had gathered fame by his iconic works of boat building and became a favorite of many customers in that industry. He then started considering retirement. As he was embarking on a journey, he told the trusted apprentice, "...as you know, I'm getting old and would soon retire."

The Builder continued, "I want to leave a legacy by building just one more boat which would be iconic and of a great value... Get this boat built and when I come back, I would retire soon afterward." "Oh, that'll be great! Consider it done, master." The apprentice responded.

The builder inspected the newly built last-to-be boat but was incredibly sad to discover that the boat was poorly built. The apprentice had used inferior materials and unjustly profited from the remainder of the money meant for a valuable boat. The boat was flabby, poor, and next to being worthless. *This is a good opportunity for me to make gain for myself*, the apprentice had thought.

Then the reward time came. "Here is the key to the boat," the Builder told the apprentice. He went on, "I had planned to present this boat as a reward for your great services to this company. Take it, it's all yours." The apprentice broke down in regret, "had I known, I would have built a better boat."

As you improve your skills and expand your skill sets, it is important to develop or improve on godly character. Character is everything to success. When money is lost, nothing is lost. When health is bad something is missing. But just as when life is lost, when sound character is lost, everything is lost. Develop a sound character laced with healthy habits, values, and virtues to complement all you've got.

Then, you will have good success!

SKILLS TO CULTIVATE

The reality of the 21st century's rapid industrialization and information technology craze come with dramatically increased competitions, unforeseen risks and dangers relating to natural and atmospheric conditions, and the need for self-improvements.

For example, with Covid-19 came unprecedented job loss for many and most corporations resorted to adopting online technologies and platforms to conduct their businesses. For people and businesses who were behind in their adaptation of information technology, it was an even more harrowing experience.

Global warming is here. The ozone layer is getting depleted, and the world is experiencing greenhouse effects. Natural disasters are looming, and many experts and scientists have begun to theorize on the global implications of this ecological deterioration. All of these are telling us to stretch ourselves, especially our minds, to find alternative means of adaptations – which might be unrealistic without new improved skills.

> If we must beat the overwhelming challenges of our generation, then we must innovate. With innovation, there'll be increased efficiency, competition, and of course, profitability must follow.

I want to believe that the next global economic outlook would prominently feature the organizations and nations that utilize computers, informational technology, and automation, otherwise, industrialization would be deflated just as competitive advantages become elusive. Even local raw materials would be greatly depleted due to inefficiency attributable to dearth or lack of innovation.

Artificial intelligence and robotics are making huge interventions in human fields and relationships with environment but there's a lot to learn and do on this. Since computers and automation are fast taking over human roles, we need to be sure that important aspects of human responsibilities and relations are not compromised by these technological substitutions.

In an article written by Emma Berthold[8], he quoted Prof. Toby Walsh who said, "…We need to get better at knowing how to teach machines before giving them too much responsibility. Once we do, the benefits to society will be immense—and we can already see real-world examples of how AI is improving our lives."

Berthold further quoted Prof. Walsh, "We should think very carefully about what it is to be fair and what it means to make a good decision... 'What does it mean mathematically for a computer program to be fair—not to be racist, ageist, or sexist? These are challenging research questions that we're now facing, as we hand these decisions to machines."

What then do we need to do? Prof. Walsh gave a clue:

> "We need to work out, as a society, how to support people as they re-skill to keep ahead of machines… 'We're going to be using technologies in 30 years' time that were invented in 20 years' time. We're going to have to do lifelong learning and pick up those skills as we go along."[9]

So, let's discuss some of the skills to cultivate to make our lives and world better.

COGNITIVE AND NON-COGNITIVE SKILLS

Both cognitive and non-cognitive skills are important to success.

Cognitive skill is "the ability of an individual to perform the various mental activities most closely associated with learning and problem solving."

"Non-cognitive skills are defined as the "patterns of thought, feelings and behaviours" (Borghans et al., 2008) that are socially determined and can be developed throughout the lifetime to produce value. Non-cognitive skills comprise personal traits, attitudes and motivations."[10]

According to a new study, "Non-cognitive skills and cognitive abilities are both important contributors to educational attainment — the number of years of formal schooling that a person completes — and lead to success across the life course."

The research found out that, "...non-cognitive skills contributed just as much to the heritability of educational attainment as cognitive ability."[11]

Let's hang our balance on cognitive skills.

The law of craft somehow finds a blend through the mechanism of cognitive skills which embrace the "domains of perception, memory, learning, attention, decision making, and language abilities."

Essentially, the value of cognitive skill lies in its thoughts processing capacity. Because everything begins with your thoughts process, we must leverage on the importance of cognitive skill in our school curricula and vocational studies. Cognitive skills help you to use the information and knowledge already acquired to solve problems.

Acquiring cognitive skills formally could be learning new trade or business, going to school to get new diploma or degrees, or getting some certifications in your chosen field. This helps you to cope with the changing trends professionally and personally.

PLANNING SKILL

Simply put, planning is the process or method of deciding or arriving at a course of action. The fact that it is a *process* means that certain types of skills are needed to produce desired excellent results.

Planning is when there's a prearranged order of future events such that administration and management of resources are seamless. Planning avoids waste of time, resources, prevents haphazard and substandard performance as it makes the future to be reasonably predictable.

To productively deploy your planning skill, you must prioritize what is important and make your goals SMART (scalable, measurable, accurate, realistic, and timely).

You must do first thing first. When he became the Prime Minister in Egypt, Joseph conducted feasibility study first and gathered right information first before building his plan for the future.

> The future that's not planned, is planned to be doomed by any type of misfortune. An unplanned life is not worth living because one would be open to the beck and calls of myriads of distractions that would eventually grind one to a halt. What is more, life becomes grotesque and phenomenally loathed with errors and confusions, the very recipes for failures!

Three types of planning skills are discernible – hindsight, insight, and foresight.

Hindsight

Hindsight is a *retrospection* that makes you to consider past trajectory of events that culminated in or contributed to your current condition. It is reflecting on past incidents to birth decisions or directions required to pursue or flow in the direction of your goals. With hindsight, I ask, "why or how did you get here?" In this regard, it is important that you master and practice the principle of evaluation discussed under the law of question.

This helped the *prodigal son* when he "came to his senses", and said, "…How many of my father's hired servants have food to spare, and here I am starving to death! I will set out and go back to my father and say to him: Father, I have sinned against heaven and against you." (Lk 15:17-18).

Insight

Insight is when you have an unusual understanding of a thing, person, or place. This "uncommon sense" gives you an added advantage in your discipline, endeavors, or quest to get unstuck. The more of *introspection* you have of a thing, the more insight you gain, and this gets you close to your goal by more than a half.

A great resource that provides the richest of insights is God's words — *logos (written)* and *rhema (revealed)*. You can also gain insights by reading and meditating on other books and literatures related to your discipline and profession.

Foresight

Foresight is the prudence or wisdom for planning. Literally, it's seeing the necessities of the future at the present time. It is the ability to see the future before it arrives. It's a way of looking into the future with the eyes of the mind, *to solve forward* human problems before they arise.

Foresight is engaging the power of vision to create the future through planning. It helps you to plan proactively. As the Bible says, "If a snake bites before you charm it, what's the use of being a snake charmer?" (Eccl 10:11, NLT).

Foresight may be premised upon some factors such as past or current experiences, future projections or purely out of necessities. And necessities, they say, is the mother of inventions.

Necessity was the basis of Joseph's foresight when he got Egypt unstuck from famine.

Family Planning – marriage and birth

The consideration on whether to have your own family (spouse and children) is planning. If you decide to have one, you must plan for it or else success becomes elusive. It is difficult if not impossible, to fulfil your purpose in life in a relationship or family unit that is full of violence, recrimination, distrust, and constant unresolved frictions.

If you chose to have children, it is important to plan *when* to have them. In some cultures, couples often begin to have kids immediately after marriage. I understand this decision is not unconnected with family pressure and what is considered "late marriages".

In other cultures, the prevalent practice is for couple to spend the first few years of marriage with each other without having children. They believe this would foster bonding, give opportunity for intimate relationship and to build the financial and emotional stability necessary to cope with attendant challenges of procreation and parenting.

It is important to work with what works for you in fear of God. The impact of unplanned family is not worth it. Proverbs 14:15 says, "… the prudent one thinks before acting." (ISV).

Family Planning – making a Will

Family planning also includes writing a will or codicil. A will is a testamentary document that sets out how your property would be distributed upon death. A codicil is an amendment to an existing will.

Apart from the fact that this puts your mind at rest regarding "who gets what", it also prevents unhealthy rivalry and litigations after your death. If you must leave anything at death, it should not be chaos. Proverbs 13:22 says, "When a good man dies, he leaves an inheritance to his grandchildren…" (TLB).

The blend of all the elements of planning skills results in success because, "by wisdom a house is built, and through understanding it is established; through knowledge its rooms are filled with rare and beautiful treasures". (Prov 23:3-4, NIV).

MANAGEMENT SKILL

Management is the prudent use of available resources to achieve a goal or sustain a process. This includes process of supervising or administering a task to ensure success. The fact is that no one is born to manage. It is a skill that must be learnt and this is where requisite leadership skills are important.

Even if useful resources are available, maladministration (poor management), wrong timing of actions or responses might waste the available resources as well as prove all efforts counterproductive. This is where management skill becomes important. With it, you bring the current certainty into the uncertain future by using the combination of hindsight, insight, and foresight to plan and create a future from the moment.

Earlier in this chapter we talked about planning skill which sets activities and tasks in motion. But where management skill is lacking, the available resources – commodities, personnel, tools, and technologies – become wasted and success becomes unrealistic. Management is the skill to prudently work out the blueprints.

Controlled spending and savings

The management skill areas include controlled spending pattern and savings.

An important component of management is savings culture. Keeping a savings habit or culture is not easy for most people and this makes management skill particularly important. However, nobody needs special knowledge on spending. Some people finish spending their salaries the first week of the new month.

It takes discipline to delay gratification and it's worthwhile in the end. "Wise people live in wealth and luxury, but stupid people spend their money as fast as they get it." (Prov 21:20, GNT).

Investing

Closely related to savings skill is investing.

Investment is putting down money or money's worth (asset) with the goal of income or profit making over a period of time.

Jesus taught many finance and business principles while he was on earth. One of them was in Matthew (Chapter 25) where half of the chapter was devoted to the principle of investment.

The master gave his three servants a capital sum for investment according to their respective abilities. The first got five thousand dollars, the second got two thousand dollars while the third got one thousand dollars. The first doubled the capital in rate of returns and was promoted to be a partner. The second also doubled the capital in rate of returns and was promoted to be a partner.

The third did not invest with his capital but rather dug a hole and kept it underground. He later accused the master of being mean. Here is the verdict. "The master was furious. 'That's a terrible way to live! It's criminal to live cautiously like that! If you knew I was after the best, why did you do less than the least? The least you could have done would have been to invest the sum with the bankers, where at least I would have gotten a little interest." (Matt 25:26-27, MSG).

That's a good lesson, isn't it?

RELATIONSHIP SKILL

Your relationship skill determines how far you go in life. This is how you relate with people and how to network and sustain your relationship with others.

Moreover, you must plan with smart people and surround yourself with vision runners who are ready, willing, and able. Learn from Joseph, David, Jesus, and Apostle Paul.

BLENDING CRAFTSMANSHIP WITH OTHER VIRTUES

Let's conclude this chapter by blending David's success skills with Jacob's.

It's important to blend your skills with creativity, originality, adaptation, and sound character. I said much about this, few pages back when I stated that skills alone are not enough.

David developed his winning skills in his experiences and relationship with God who taught him how to fight. As a faithful herder, he made integrity his watchword as he fought lion and bear with bare hands to mitigate risk and save cost. His improved skill led to his victory over Goliath.

To be clear, David was not the only person who killed lion with bare hands. Samson did the same (See Judges 14:6). But instead of improving this special skill, Samson drained himself with self-indulgence and died in a questionable way. David improved on his skill and killed Goliath. Jacob improved his management skill and God prospered him greatly.

> *Talents, giftings or skills without prompt action or sound character, are like birds without wings or crabs without limbs. They cripple you into failures.*

I randomly came across a video on social media sometimes in 2020 where a guy was using his toes to play piano. And my comment was that, as long as man continued to exert the power of imagination and think productively, the world will continue to advance.

Cultivate new skills, improve on them, blend them with sound character and ask for God's favor.

You'll be unstuck!

Amen!

11

GIVE YOUR OBSTACLE A PROPER LABEL

Mastering the Law of Perspective

"Your servant has killed both the lion and the bear; and this uncircumcised Philistine will be like one of them, since he has taunted and defied the armies of the living God."

- I Samuel 17:36, AMP

"Some people see the glass half full. Others see it half empty. I see a glass that's twice as big as it needs to be."

- George Carlin

"Yesterday I was sad, today I am happy! Yesterday I had a problem, today I still have the same problem! But today I changed the way I look at it!"

- C. JoyBell C.

During one of my classes in college, one of my Professors was trying to emphasize one of the problems associated with law as a concept which is elusiveness. He had taught us that there was no specific definition to foreclose all definitions of law and identified scholars in the field of jurisprudence such as Paton, Roscoe Pound, Savigny and others.

Notably, every definition hinged on author's abstractions, verbal slangs, or perspectives which ultimately meant that law had no consensus definition. He then ended with the following story by an ancient writer.

> It was six men of Indostan to learning much inclined, who went to see the Elephant
> (Though all of them were blind), That each by observation Might satisfy his mind.
>
> The *First* approached the Elephant and happening to fall Against his broad and sturdy side,
> At once began to bawl: "God bless me! but the Elephant Is very like a WALL!"
>
> The *Second*, feeling of the tusk, Cried, "Ho, what have we here, So very round and smooth and sharp? To me 'tis mighty clear This wonder of an Elephant Is very like a SPEAR!"
>
> The *Third* approached the animal and happening to take the squirming trunk within his hands,
> Thus boldly up and spake: "I see," quoth he, "the Elephant Is very like a SNAKE!"
>
> The *Fourth* reached out an eager hand and felt about the knee "What most this wondrous beast is like Is mighty plain, quoth he: "Tis clear enough the Elephant Is very like a TREE!"
>
> The *Fifth*, who chanced to touch the ear, said: "E'en the blindest man can tell what this resembles most; Deny the fact who can, this marvel of an Elephant Is very like a FAN!"
>
> The Sixth no sooner had begun About the beast to grope, than seizing on the swinging tail That fell within his scope, "I see," quoth he, "the Elephant Is very like a ROPE!"
>
> And so these men of Indostan disputed loud and long, each in his own opinion
> exceeding stiff and strong, though each was partly in the right, and all were in the wrong!"[1]

As discernible from the Indostan blind men's story, your perspectives of events of your life – including your problems, obstacles, challenges – impact your life significantly.

LAW OF PERSPECTIVE

The law of perspective states that *your problems are as real as your perspectives*. Your perspective is your reality or conclusion drawn from variable factors including, environment, experiences, knowledge, and values.

What you say, do or think is a matter of perspective. In the arena of the valley of Ella, we see one subject matter (Goliath's threat) but two different perspectives. All the men of Israel saw obstacle in Goliath and ran away in trepidation. (I Sam 17:24). David however saw Goliath as an opportunity to teach the world a lesson that *no one defies "the armies of the living God" and goes scot-free.*

Your problems are your perspectives, and your perspectives are your problems.

> The gap between you and your problems (or solutions) are the prism or lens of interpretation, and of course, the meanings attached to your perspectives.

For example, the gap between whether Lazarus was dead was the *lens of interpretations* of Mary and Martha, which sharply contrasted with that of Jesus. Mary and Martha saw death and sorrow. Jesus saw sleep and glorification of his father in heaven.

OTHERS SAW DEATH, JESUS SAW SLEEP...

Mary and Martha, Lazarus' sisters had sent a message to Jesus that his friend, Lazarus, was sick, "Lord, the one you love is sick." (Jn

11:3, NIV). Jesus replied with a tone of hope and assurance that the "sickness will not end in death…" (v4). Jesus delayed for two more days. Lazarus later died. Jesus saw sleep where others saw death.

"Then he said, "Our friend Lazarus has fallen asleep, but now I will go and wake him up." The disciples said, "Lord, if he is sleeping, he will soon get better!" They thought Jesus meant Lazarus was simply sleeping, but Jesus meant Lazarus had died. So he told them plainly, "Lazarus is dead. And for your sakes, I'm glad I wasn't there, for now you will really believe. Come, let's go see him." Thomas, nicknamed the Twin, said to his fellow disciples, "Let's go, too—and die with Jesus." (Jn 11:11-16, NLT).

As far as Lazarus' family and the entire mourners were concerned, Lazarus was hopelessly dead. *Their default knowledge had informed them that the hope of seeing a person that is medically certified dead was lost and this knowledge impacted on their perspective which was not hidden in their conversation with Jesus.*

Do not blame the mourners, we are all alike. We've had our knowledge shape our perspectives about life. We've had our lives, hopes, and dreams limited by our perspectives. We begin to live under the influence of premature conclusions. *"Since our prayers seemed unanswered"* even when coupled with fasting and sanctimonious deeds and moral virtues, and *"it appears Jesus is more delayed than expected"* in our case, we draw a warped conclusion that our dreams and bright future are *"dead"*.

But Jesus restored Lazarus to life at the *timing* that would glorify God!

The good news is this: Jesus only sees "sleep" in our "dead situations." He might not have shown up at our most painful moments, a good perspective should be that his delay is not a denial. It's just that his measurement of timing is different than ours and this explains our internal conflicts and narrow-

mindedness when faced with tough situations. The Bible says, "God is our refuge and strength, a very present help in trouble." (Ps 46:1, ESV). He is the "present help" according to his own interpretation of time and season.

RECOLLECT AND RENAME ...

You can recollect your experiences, rename, and have them conform to what gives you a godly perspective that will inspire you to move ahead despite besetting odds. Rename them with positive tags such that each time you look at what came as obstacles, all you see is motivation to look forward to achieving your purpose.

In Genesis 32:24, Jacob was left alone in the night of his encounter with the angel of God, but he was never the same again. Jacob lost his hip joint to the encounter which could have made him to label the place something like "brutal", "nasty", "damning", and the likes. But his experiences over the years plus the current one had taught him to choose a brighter side when life presented both bleak and not so bleak conditions.

Jacob instead named the place Peniel believing that he saw God face-to-face but his life was spared.

I suggest that you develop motivating expressions and vocabularies such as this challenge is *"my next ride to success"*, *"the current challenge before me now is..."*, *"I will survive this"*, *"My future is better than this experience"*, *"I will succeed"*, *"I will not die in this..."*.

A PROPER LABEL

Perhaps one of the best illustrations of the law of perspective is captured by the words of the spies who came to Moses with negative reports.

> "But the men who had gone up with him said, "We are not able to go up against the people [of Canaan], for they

are too strong for us." So they gave the Israelites a bad report about the land which they had spied out, saying, "The land through which we went, in spying it out, is a land that devours its inhabitants. And all the people that we saw in it are men of great stature. There we saw the Nephilim (the sons of Anak are part of the Nephilim); and we were like grasshoppers in our own sight, and so we were in their sight."

- Num 13:31-33 (AMP)

Most of the spies were victims of negative perspectives with lower estimations of themselves and their abilities. They had a poor perspective of what God had endowed them with and their inner eye of assessment was miserably dimmed by the physical size of their obstacles.

By contrast, David described Goliath as an *uncircumcised Philistine.* This label goes to the root of David's victory because Goliath was outside of the covenant that God made with the Israelites, that every male among them should be circumcised on the eight day (See Genesis 17:10-12). Goliath was already in the position of an enemy of God.

> You've got to properly label what is confronting you in the light of the power of the Almighty God.

RIGHT PERSPECTIVE, WISE INTERPRETATION

Right interpretation of times helps you to form and understand the purpose of a season and this understanding invariably affects your perspective on what is priority to you, what stands as a problem, or an opportunity during the time in question.

"He also said to the crowds, "When you see a cloud rising in the west, you immediately say, 'It is going to rain,' and that is how it turns out. And when [you see that] a south wind is blowing, you say, 'It will be a hot day,' and it happens. You hypocrites (play-actors, pretenders)! You know how to analyze *and* intelligently interpret the appearance of the earth and sky [to forecast the weather], but why do you not intelligently interpret this present time?"

- Lk 12:54-56, AMP

When God's will is your overriding perspective of what you're passing through, you can't but get correct, godly, and unmistakably true inter-pretations. This is wisdom. (see I Corinthians 2:6-8).

Your perspective would be right when your sense of interpretation is right, especially with the *kairos* approach which interprets events based on meanings or values you get out of time rather than length. This is where I agree with Stephen R Covey, et al.

"...But there are entire cultures in the world that approach life from a Kairos-an "appropriate time" or "quality time"-paradigm. Time is something to be experienced. It's exponential, existential. The essence of Kairos time is how much value you get out of it rather than how much chronos time you put into it. Our language reflects recognition of Kairos time when we ask, "Did you have a good time?" We're not asking about the amount of chronos time spent in a particular way, but about the value, the quality, of that time."[2]

When you have the authentic wisdom of Christ Jesus, you are rightly positioned for success, victory, and freedom from all oppressions. This is because, "...no one may deceive you by fine-sounding arguments." (Col 2:5, NIV).

YOUR PERSPECTIVE DETERMINES YOUR REQUEST

In Acts of the Apostles 3:1-6, we see a crippled beggar whose perspective of his problems determined his request. He was begging for alms, a temporary fix, instead of asking to be healed and restored.

Peter, who understood the principle of perspective, used it to get the beggar unstuck. In verse four, Peter redirected the beggar to *"look at us"*. And what's the result? The beggar obeyed, changed his direction, was ministered to, and got more than what he begged for. He had begged for alms so he could maintain his status quo, but he got a permanent fix by receiving healing to stand on his feet.

The Psalmist once said, *"I look up to the mountains; does my strength come from mountains? No, my strength comes from GOD, who made heaven, and earth, and mountains"* (Ps 121:1-2, MSG). What a perspective!

> To succeed, it is necessary to have a paradigm shift; a shift in the worldview of what's standing against you. A paradigm shift is a change in the way you look at a thing, especially a problem.

In his bestselling book titled *"the 7 Habits of Highly Effective People"*, Stephen R. Covey discussed the importance of a paradigm shift. According to the famous author,

> *Each of us tends to think we see things as they are, that we are objective. But this is not the case. We see the world, not as it is, but as we are - or, as we are conditioned to see it. When we open our mouths to describe what we see, we in effect describe ourselves, our perceptions, our paradigms. When other people disagree with us, we immediately think something is wrong with them.... sincere, clearheaded people see things differently, each looking through the unique lens of experience...But each person's interpretation of these facts represents prior experiences, and the facts have no meaning whatsoever apart from the interpretation.*[3]

196

Like David, you must make a paradigm shift, first, in your mind by creating a victory or success worldview. The crippled beggar obviously lacked this shift and remained stuck in poverty, neglect, and shame, for long time in his life.

PERSPECTIVE TRIGGERS

I want you to take a moment and read this story I heard years ago.

"There was once a man who had four sons. He wanted to teach his sons not to judge too fast and not to give up easily. So, he sent each one of the boys on their way to the same pear tree that was far from their village. The first son had to go in the winter, the second in the spring, the third in the summer, and the youngest son in the autumn. When everyone had visited the tree and returned, the father gathered them and asked them to describe what they saw.

The first son said the tree was ugly, bent, and distorted. The second son said that it was not possible to be the same tree he had found - he had seen a tree covered with green buds and a promise of fertility. The third son said that what his brothers saw was not the tree - he saw the pear all blooming and radiant, spreading sweet aroma, the tree was so beautiful that it seemed to him to be the most beautiful tree he has ever seen. The youngest son said he saw a totally different tree – full of fruits all over, a symbol of complete life and satisfaction.

The father listened to the stories of his sons and told them that each of them was right and they all saw the same tree. Just every boy has visited the pear during a different season of the year. That was also the lesson he wanted to convey to them - one cannot judge both the trees and the people for one season. Their true nature - as well as the joy and love they bring - is a result we can only see at the end of the year when all the seasons have passed."

The story concluded with some advice. "If you decide to opt out in the winter, you will miss the promise of a new life that comes with spring; the beauty and warmth of the summer; and the abundance of autumn. Do not let the pain and difficulty of a season or period of your life destroy your long-term happiness."[4]

With that said, let's discuss some of the factors that influence your perspectives (perspective triggers).

1. Encounters with God and revelations received: Our encounters with God never leave us the same as their outcomes greatly affect our viewpoints of life and its attendant troubles.

For some, such encounters completely change their perspectives of their problems such that they no longer see those negative experiences as problems but as mere *unusual blend of life*, *temporary interruptions in life*, or as absolutely *nothing to worry about.*

Paul's bitter suffering episodes in II Cor 11:23-29 are enough to make a person give up and lose hope. But not Apostle Paul! The more he was pummeled with the rod of afflictions, the more he sought to have encounters with God. His encounters with God of grace changed his perspective on his sufferings: "…I am most happy, then, to be proud of my weaknesses, in order to feel the protection of Christ's power over me. I am content with weaknesses, insults, hardships, persecutions, and difficulties for Christ's sake. For when I am weak, then I am strong." (I Cor 12:7-10).

In fact, he described his perspective of all his sufferings as *"momentary, light distress [this passing trouble]"* and this helped him to get unstuck as he completed his race on earth victoriously. He said, "I have fought the good fight, I have finished the race, I have kept the faith." (II Tim 4:7, NCV).

> In your travails, get closer to God;
> He will give you encounters that
> would change your perspectives of
> your afflictions.

2. Experiences (yours and others'): Like any other person, you are a product of experiences, either of yours or of others, especially your parents and family members. It is your interpretation of the perspectives formed in those experiences that informs your decisions or actions thereafter.

Lysa Terkeurst carried the heavy weight of pain from her husband's extramarital affair for a long time. Then she chose to forgive her husband. While healing (and "connecting the dots") from this emotional wound, she realized that her husband, Art, was *"raised with the belief that emotion was intensely private and better kept to oneself."* Lysa said that her husband *"grew up in a house where feelings weren't expressed. So he learnt to keep secrets"* contrary to her experience where *"every feeling was not just expressed but declared loudly and processed loudly."*[5]

Art's childhood experience was not only part of him, but also shaped his perspective, such that he rarely expressed "negative" emotions to Lysa.

Life's experiences never leave you the same. Lysa later consciously formed a perspective that was shaped from Genesis 1:27 where the Bible stated that God formed mankind in His own image and began to process on her husband's affair with a different lens: *"The affair, while it is a reality, is not his identity. He's a child of God whom I can forgive."*[6]

This is a paradigm shift!

She told a story of her friend named Colette trying to connect the dots from her past. Colette dreaded sunrises and sunsets and would not want to see them.

Colette recollected that growing up as a child, morning and night times were threats to her for reasons outside of her control. 'So her belief system that formed as a child was that these two times of the day were to be avoided, not enjoyed." Happily, as Colette "connected these dots, she realized she needed to correct her belief about sunrises and sunsets."

Like Colette, I suggest you reflect, connect the past dots, and correct the wrongs ones.

Paul says that, you should *do* your "best by filling your minds and meditating on things true, noble, reputable, authentic, compelling, gracious—the best, not the worst; the beautiful, not the ugly; things to praise, not things to curse..." (Phil 4:8-9, MSG).

Your positive mindset on these things is one of the surest ways to get unstuck from cycles of afflictions.

Let your experiences give you positive perspectives that move you ahead.

3. Sense of interpretation: To a large extent, your sense of interpretation defines not only how far you go in life but also whether you'll fulfill your dreams ultimately. How do you interpret events of life when you are befuddled with unusual blend of life? Are you limited by the traditional five senses of taste, smell, hearing, feeling, and seeing?

The fact is that no one really amounts to any meaningful person who is roundly limited by five senses. Everyone is a genius. Albert Einstein said, "But if you judge a fish on its ability to climb a tree, it will live its whole life believing that it is stupid."

The Spirit of God inside of you is your spiritual eyes to see things from spiritual (God's) perspective because "God has given us his Spirit. That's why we don't think the same way that the people of this world think. That's also why we can recognize the blessings that God has given us." (I Cor 2:12, CEV). This is called a *Holy or Sanctified Sense*!

You cannot understand or form a godly perspective of your condition if you don't have the Spirit of God (Holy Spirit) (See I Corithains 2:14).

> It is the wrong interpretation of your unique abilities that sends you on a frolic of unhealthy jealousy and mis-guided competitions.

There is no point for competition when it comes to divine purpose, and every purpose attracts its distinctive thorns and unique glory. When you have poor reflections and warped perspectives of "thorns" associated with your purpose, envy sets in.

Many of us are like Isaac; we never get unstuck until we develop a godly habit of forming positive perspective of our situations and tag them with the description of possibilities, success, victories, and prosperity. He called the place Rehoboth where he settled and flourished. (See Genesis 26:22). This sharply contrasted with his earlier places named after his former experiences – Esek and sitnah.

You don't have to experiment with the one life that you've got before you get unstuck! Interpret your experiences in line with God's purpose for your life. Use your *Holy sense!*

Form a conqueror's perspective because "In everything we have won more than a victory because of Christ who loves us." (Rom 8:37, CEV).

4. Imagination: Our minds are powerful tools to create worlds of ideas and images to form any type of perspectives. It's like you are given a plain sheet of paper and a pen and asked to write whatever you want there. It is up to you on what to write.

Your imagination has everything to do with your life- present and future. Its productive use connects you to victory and success.

God worked through Abram's imagination.

Abram was stuck with childlessness. That was a big deal for an octogenarian who had a septuagenarian wife. God had promised to be his exceeding reward and to give him a son at an old age. He obviously needed help connecting the promise to reality as it was hard to conceive let alone believe such a thing. The promise seemed unrealistic, right?

God then helped him to form a different perspective about having many children, by leading him out saying, "Look at the sky and see if you can count the stars. That's how many descendants you will have." Abram believed the LORD, and the LORD was pleased with him." (Gen 15:5-6, CEV).

Essentially what God did was to scan the image of the future and program it into Abram's software (imagination), knowing that this will auto-process in his mind and thus help him to form a blissful perspective of a man with many children. That's what happened eventually!

Your imagination is the field where "nations" are *imagined* and *imaged*. This may sound like a pun or slogan, but it is nonetheless true because it doesn't only make literal sense but also Biblical sense.

God personally led Abram to imprint "image of nations" into Abram's mind when He asked him to count the numbers of stars in the sky and then promised him, *"...That's how many descendants you will have...".* This promise was later fulfilled but not without initial "imaging" in Abram's mind. This perspective somehow helped him to endure many problems which would have stuck him to failure.

As powerful as your imagination is, in activating your perspective, it does not limit God even though God would not deny its constructive usage. God knew that Abram's mind was a good *material* to use for his blessings, he asked him to begin a mental exercise of counting the stars.

From the time God promised to make Abram father of many nations, Abram was already elevated to that status in the spiritual realm. But it would not manifest physically until the revelation is caught, conceived, and processed in his mind into physical realities. Like Abram, David conceived in his mind, to fight and kill Goliath. Once this perspective was formed, all his motivations and energies moved in that direction.

God wants you to use your imagination first to *receive* revelations from Him, and then to *conceive* and *process* them to create a better future for you, and by extension, to create a better world than you met it.

---

5. Historical Factors: Until we reach about eight to ten years, we mostly do what our parents and older siblings do; what they told us, internalizing and imitating how they talked, acted, and reacted. We unconsciously picked up all these when growing up and formed certain perspectives about issues of life and life itself based on what they told us.

Many people continued in that default mode, unfortunately. That's why you must be careful what and how you learn and learn the right thing from your elders and parents, otherwise you might form a wrong, ungodly perspective from them and miss out on your purpose.

Apostle Peter said, "... in the past you were living in a worthless way, a way passed down from the people who lived before you. But you were saved from that useless life. You were bought, not with something that ruins like gold or silver." (I Pet 1:18, NCV).

203

But like Apostle Paul, we must *"put away childish things..."* when we grow up. (See I Corinthians 13:11).

6. Environment: Your environment is not just the physical or geographical. It includes the people you hang out with – friends, family, peers, or colleagues. A toxic environment is a bad place to live because the probability is high that you'll be infected with the negativity that is rife around you.

Children who grow up in bad environments tend to see life from a warped or crooked perspective. They often refuse to take responsibility for their actions (or inactions) and blame others for their woes, becoming despondent about the future. Therefore, they are either criminally-minded or hang around criminal people. Either way, they're already being perceived by the public as socially delinquent and disreputable.

Many good guys are behind bars across the world and even several innocent people have had to pay the supreme price for what they did not do. But the fact that the public has already identified them with bad guys makes it difficult for them to overcome the past just as it is to move ahead. You want to avoid bad environment at all costs because it may cost you a lot to move ahead in life in such companies.

FIX YOUR LENS NOW

Now, let's wrap up our discussions on the law of perspective. We've talked so much about it and so what do you do next? I suggest you start a clinical demonstration and fix your lens.

The scientific knowledge of optical physics tells us about having one image that may be seen differently using different external applications. An image may have aberrations or clarity depending on the type of mirror and mechanics carried out on the mirror. When we view an object through a concave mirror and a parabolic mirror, we would get different results – blurred, clear, or magnified.

Imagine that you have a few incident rays of light on a parallel travel from an original point to a principal axis of a concave mirror (mirror that bends inward). Unlike the other rays, the incident rays on the top and the one at the bottom would fail to pass through the focal point and reflect differently. This is a departure technically called an aberration due to the spherical nature of the concave mirror.

To correct the aberration, a candle-object demonstration is carried out where the outer edges of the demonstration mirror is covered to make the image more focused and clearer (correction of blurriness or spherical aberration). To get this clear result, concave mirror is substituted for a parabolic mirror which has a significant shape.

The impact of the parabolic mirror in correcting spherical aberrations is a typology of wisdom of the law of perspective. It's like collecting the dots of your life experiences, connecting with them introspectively, and choosing to form a positive perspective of them in a way that connects you with the future of your dream.

Interestingly, you have the responsibility to form the winning perspectives because it's an internal work. You can do this when you honestly evaluate, sincerely acknowledge your limitations, and totally depend on God for the ultimate victory.

In the words of Lysa Terkeurst,

> *At the very time we grieve a loss, we gain more and more awareness of an eternal perspective. Grieving is such a deep work and a long process, it feels like we might not survive it. But eventually we do. And even though we still may never agree on this side of eternity that the trade the good God gave us is worth what we've lost, we hold on to hope by trusting God. Everything lost that we placed in the hands of God isn't a forever loss…God took Adam's bone. He gave him back the gift of a woman."[7]*

What a perspective!

David properly labelled Goliath as uncircumcised Philistine which meant Goliath was without God's covenant cover and liable to die at any time. This realization pushed him into action and the rest is history.

Like candle-object demonstration is carried out to correct concave mirror's spherical aberration, you can turn to God's Spirit – the Holy Spirit – to help in correcting a victim's or loser's perspectives to a winner's perspective in all issues of life. Happily, the Bible says, "The spirit of man is the candle of the LORD, searching all the inward parts of the belly." (Prov 20:27).

You can use your power of choice to look at your obstacles and pains differently, even now!

12

SPEAKING FAITH AND POSITIVE CONFESSIONS

Practicing the Law of Confession and Voice Command

*"Then said David to the Philistine, Thou comest to me with a sword,
and with a spear, and with a shield: but I come to thee in the name of
the LORD of hosts, the God of the armies of Israel, whom thou
hast defied. This day will the LORD deliver thee into mine hand; and I
will smite thee, and take thine head from thee; and I will give the carcases of
the host of the Philistines this day unto the fowls of the air, and to the wild
beasts of the earth; that all the earth may know that there is a God in Israel.
And all this assembly shall know that the LORD saveth not with sword and
spear: for the battle is the LORD's, and he will give you into our hands."*

- I Sam 17:45-47, KJV

*"God comes on his own terms. He comes when commands are revered, hearts
are clean, and confession is made"*

- Max Lucado

*"Our confession will either imprison us or set us free. Our confession is the
result of our believing, and our believing is the result of our right or wrong
thinking."*

- Kenneth E. Hagin

I recently watched an online sermon of a popular Pastor. As I could remember, he stated that words of your mouth are the clearest signs of your maturity as a Christian. To emphasize the power of words and confessions, the Pastor cited an example of a preacher during a ministration in which he had prayed for the lame who walked instantly.

Under the same strength of a powerful anointing, the preacher said, "I can die for this country...." and a lot of weighty words. According to the Pastor, the preacher was said to have been gunned down in front of his house few months later.

While I'm not aware of any immediate or remote evidence that linked the preacher's words to his death, I know as a fact that words are powerful tools that shape or reshape our lives and that words are never wasted. We just don't know when and how they will manifest.

Ignorance is not an excuse to deny non-occurrence of an event!

LAW OF CONFESSION AND VOICE COMMANDS

The law of confession and voice command (law of confession) states that *a man's confession soon becomes his reality; what a man confesses, he possesses. His constant confessions are command buttons that shape or reshape his life.*

Being a polysemic word, *confession* may mean your profession of faith or a statement of admission of guilt. In general terms, confession refers to expression or statement which may be verbal or non-verbal. One thing is clear about confession: it is a communication which may be to yourself, to another person or to no one in particular.

In the context of this chapter, confession refers to word, expression, statement, or communication howsoever expressed, that emanates from you to another, or to you.

208

David's confessions in I Sam 17:45-47 were not general motivational rhetoric but life-carrying confessions that were rooted in God's words and covenant.

YOUR FAITH IN JESUS CHRIST IS A SPEAKING FAITH.

Your faith in God is speaking faith.

You must speak out your faith to the situation. When you are in a warfare, every part of you is involved, including your mouth. "Then said David to the Philistine, Thou comest to me with a sword, and with a spear, and with a shield: but I come to thee in the name of the Lord of hosts, the God of the armies of Israel, whom thou hast defied" (I Sam 17:45).

> In the face of obstacles, you need to do more by complementing your actions with confessions of what God has said about you or your condition. Sooner or later, you become what you repeatedly speak out.

"For with the heart a person believes [in Christ as Savior] resulting in his justification [that is, being made righteous—being freed of the guilt of sin and made acceptable to God]; and with the mouth he acknowledges and confesses [his faith openly], resulting in and confirming [his] salvation. Rom 10:10, AMP

Confession to salvation here means confession that invites salvaging, rescuing you from your problems.

SPEAK TO THE MOUNTAIN DIRECTLY

David targeted his expression of faith directly at his obstacle – Goliath. Overcoming cycles of afflictions requires a well-coordinated and expressed faith. Faith not well directed, just like a weapon misdirected, cannot eliminate your obstacles.

Jesus said, "... I tell you the truth, if you have faith and don't doubt, you can do things like this and much more. You can even say to this mountain, 'May you be lifted up and thrown into the sea,' and it will happen." (Matthew 21:21, NLT).

Jesus cursed the fig tree and it dried up. When you experience failures, sicknesses, and career frustration that impede your growth, what do you say?

CONFESSION ROOTED IN GOD

The basis of the faith spoken by David against Goliath was the God of the armies of Israel and not mere empty quotations, psychological or philosophical expressions. God is committed to responding to the call to battle that is made out of child-like faith.

> God is the Word of God and the God of the Word who lives and thrives in the Word and who by the Word, spoke the world into existence. Nothing existed until He spoke the Word to create the world.

As we can see, until verse three when God said, "...let there be light...", "The earth was formless and empty, and darkness covered the deep waters..." (Gen 1:2, NLT). God believed in Himself and spoke to the empty, formless earth. And it happened – there was light! Hallelujah!

Looking through Genesis chapter 1, you'll discover that there are about *nine "And God said..."* This was not mere poetic emphasis but must have been spoken to create a *principle of voice authority* embedded in the law of confession, which posits that, *nothing works until words are spoken and nothing good happens except good words are spoken*. Genesis 1:31 clinches it all, "God looked over everything he had made; it was so good, so very good!" (MSG).

WE BELIEVE, THEREFORE WE SPEAK

II Corinthians 4:13 says, "We having the same spirit of faith, according as it is written, I believed, and therefore have I spoken; we also believe, and therefore speak;".

If you really believe in God, then you would speak out what you believe. You would speak out success and not failure; victory and not defeat; good health and not bad health, breakthrough and not stagnation. Check it out, every creature you can see or imagine was created by *spoken word*.

> "In the beginning was the Word, and the Word was with God, and the Word was God. The same was in the beginning with God. All things were made by him: and without him was not anything made that was made. In him was life; and the life was the light of men. And the light shineth in darkness; and the darkness comprehended it not".
>
> - Jn 1:1-5

David's faith was rooted in the God of the armies of Israel, and this clearly reflected in his words, **"I come to thee in the name of the LORD of hosts, the God of the armies of Israel."** To be clear, David was a man of skills in battles and chronicles of victory experiences but as helpful and needed those skills and experiences were, David did not repose his faith in them. To him, they were of collateral importance.

As powerful as King Saul's armor was imagined to be, David's faith was not rooted in them. God "...does not delight in the strength (military power) of the horse, nor does He take pleasure in the legs (strength) of a man. The Lord favors those who fear and worship Him [with awe-inspired reverence and obedience], Those who wait for His mercy and lovingkindness." (Ps 147:10-11, AMP).

So, David's prophesying victory over Goliath was based on nothing except God and His word. "In You, O LORD, I have placed my trust and taken refuge; Let me never be ashamed; In Your righteousness rescue me." (Ps 31:1, AMP).

EVERY WORD CARRIES WEIGHT

No word is wasted because you are responsible for every idle, negative, or positive word. "Death and life are in the power of the tongue, and those who love it and indulge it will eat its fruit and bear consequences of their words." (Prov 18:21).

God's Spirit that accompanies the word of instructions is the catalyst for the actualization of what has been spoken into existence. Isaiah 34:16 says, "… for the LORD has promised this. His Spirit will make it all come true." (NLT).

Even if the giant still appears to be imposing after you have repeatedly confessed and declared what God says about it, it is already eliminated in the spiritual realm. The physical manifestation is just a matter of time. At the time the Israelites were *shouting*, the city of Jericho was still physically lively but in the spiritual realm, it had collapsed.

When David kept confessing victory over Goliath, the latter was the still maintaining the title of a champion but in a matter of time, he became a carcass.

> Positive confessions rooted in the Scriptures are not mere motivational or emotional expressions, but powerful in God to demolish stronghold and arguments that tend to pull you away from success and victory.

That's why you must be rooted in God's words such that your mind and mouth are full of the word of authority. "Remember what

Christ taught, and let his words enrich your lives and make you wise...." (Col 3:16, TLB).

The power in the word of God flows through your confessions which then carries spiritual weight to demolish obstacles.

I have sat many times under the teachings of Pastor Sam Adeyemi of Daystar Christian Center, Lagos, Nigeria. He has a special grace in easy delivery of his message to millions of his viewers globally.

One day he said, "...*the Word of God in your mouth is as powerful as the Word of God in God's mouth.*" How amazing that is! I am yet to recover from the revelation I caught through that statement.

One of the revelations I got that day was that, as long as I have a right standing with God and I stand on the principles of His word, if I speak God's word concerning my situations then I would get what God promised at the time when God wants me to have it. So, I know that, standing on God's word, I cannot fail because by the word, the world was framed. Indeed, speaking faith is winning faith!

YOUR TONGUE AS A WEAPON

Unlike David who understood and used the weapon of tongue to create the victory he wanted, Naomi was either ignorant or careless about the power in her tongue. This is Naomi: "Don't call me Naomi," she responded. "Instead, call me Mara, for the Almighty has made life very bitter for me." (Ruth 1:20, NLT).

Naomi's poor perspective of her predicament blurred her reasoning and crept into her tongue when she said, *"call me Mara.."* interpreted to be, *"call me bitter."* This shouldn't be so!

Naomi could have formed a positive godly perspective that Job formed when he said, "When a tree is chopped down, there is always the hope that it will sprout again. Its roots and stump may rot, but at the touch of water, fresh twigs shoot up." (Job 14:7-9, CEV), or developed Abraham's perspective who believed that God would bring Isaac back to life if he sacrificed Isaac. (See Hebrews 11:19).

WHATEVER ADAM CALLED THEM...

When I got married, my wife and I would use different kinds of words to express our moods and feelings – some not too good!

One day God opened my eyes to Genesis 2:19 which says, "And out of the ground the Lord God formed every beast of the field, and every fowl of the air; and brought them unto Adam to see what he would call them: and whatsoever Adam called every living creature, that was the name thereof."

The last statement particularly struck me differently even though I was aware of this Bible portion before. So, I reasoned, "*whatever I call my wife is what she becomes...*". Since them I changed for good as I started calling her different good names and sweet nicknames.

The law of confession is a transforming principle that can create a different new world or future for you, depending on how you use it. This law somehow correlates with the law of perspective discussed in chapter eleven, in that, when you form a positive perspective of the problem confronting you, the next thing you do is to speak forth what you want to happen – speak the formed perspective into reality.

After He had imagined that a man should be formed after His likeness, God took a step further and "... said "Let us make man in our image, after our likeness..." (Gen 1:26). This is the law of confession in its purest form. It's because of *"God said..."* that you are formed into a human being!

> After God had done His part of creation, He asked Adam to share the privilege of being "co-creator" with God and the privilege of exercising the authority he had given to man – authority to declare things into existence, asking him to name the creation.

What do you call your spouse? How do you describe your current relationships? What are you saying about your wayward kids or their addiction to bad behaviors? What are your confessions about your future or your health, career, and ministry?

SPEAK TO DRY BONES

During his afflictions, Job lamented that his spirit was broken and that his days were cut short as grave awaited him. (Job 17:11). While still in distress, he queried, "And where is now my hope? as for my hope, who shall see it?" (Job 17:15).

Like the Israelites who dispersed at the threats of Goliath, the generations that followed Job had similar experiences and *imagined themselves cut off.* Jeremiah was one of them when he lamented that *he thought he was about to be cut off but that he called the name of God who answered him.* (See Lamentation 3:54-56). In other words, they were stuck in restraints.

God depicted the house of Israel as dry bones and was determined to revive them but not without applying His proven agelong principle of law of confession. He had to summon Prophet Ezekiel by His Spirit and commanded him to speak, prophesy and declare revival and life into the dry bones – dead house of Israel.

"Again He said unto me, Prophesy upon these bones, and say unto them, O ye dry bones, hear the word of the LORD...So I prophesied as I was commanded: and as I prophesied, there was a noise, and behold a shaking, and the bones came together, bones to his bone." (Ezek 37:4-7)

The wonder of the law of confession is in the Spirit of the word spoken. Ezekiel declared what God commanded and the Spirit in the word created the wonder of restoration; he believed God and spoke out and dry bones received flesh.

God made it clear that, even though it used to be said among the Israelites that their bones had dried up within them, as Job had said in his afflictions, He would restore them to life by the power of the spoken word.

God could have commanded Ezekiel to do some other things like imagining the dry bones being miraculously covered with flesh. But He chose to highlight the principle of voice command and confession of the word of his power by which he upholds all things. (See Hebrews 1:3).

Like the Israelites, we might as well have been walking around like pieces of dry bones even though we are dressed in the best of clothing, wearing the most expensive perfumes, and wearing the best of shoes.

But like Ezekiel, we must prophesy and speak into reality, the careers of our dream, nation of our dream, the present and future of our dreams. Righteousness exalts a nation, but sin is its reproach. Prophesy a reign of righteousness in your nation and declare peace, the fruit of righteousness. Speak good health into reality in your body and stop being carried away by doctors' reports. Speak of God's report.

According to Ezekiel, as he was prophesying, there was a noise, rattle sound, and the bones came together. Women who delivered of babies without epidural or other form of sedatives could explain the pain of childbirth. But as soon as they open their eyes, the joy of beholding the fruit of their travails soon displaces the hitherto pain.

Just like there were noises during Ezekiel's declarations, you may have to feel uneasiness and experience zero comfort level. You may experience *noises and rattling* in your mind but at the end of the day, a turning point of bliss, peace, joy, health, and fulfilment of your joy is worth waiting for.

IN-BETWEEN COMMANDS AND MANIFESTATION

Are there times when waiting sucks and you feel like throwing in the towel? Absolutely yes! You experience real life conflict when your desires conflict with experiences. What then do you do? Keep saying what God is saying about you! And keep faith alive!

After Ezekiel had prophesied into dry bones and they were covered with flesh, the best they could be was what looked like zombies or lifeless images. That's not what he wanted. He must have thought, *"of what use is flesh without breath?"*

But God wasn't done yet, just as He's not done with you. God told Ezekiel, "…Prophesy unto the wind, prophesy, son of man, and say to the wind, Thus saith the Lord GOD; Come from the four winds, O breath, and breathe upon these slain, that they may live." (Ezek 37:9). What's the result? "…breath came into them, and they lived, and stood up upon their feet, an exceeding great army." (Ezek 37:10). Amazing outcome of persistence in positive confessions!

In Mark 11:12-25, Jesus cursed a fig tree because of its fruitlessness. But the fig tree did not wither instantly. Anyone passing by would still see the tree and its heavy foliage but in the supernatural, it was as good as dead. Jesus had spoken and his word, like God's words, "...will not return ... empty..." (Is 55:11, NCV).

Don't be discouraged when the cursed "fig tree is still green" or when "the commanded giant is still talking"; this shall be your testimony: "The Lord has blessed you because you believed that he will keep his promise." (Lk 1:45, CEV).

EN HAKORE

Things don't just happen in the Kingdom of God! Jesus says, "... but now ask and keep on asking and you will receive, so that your joy may be full and complete." (Jn 16:24, AMP).

Samson was foretold to deliver Israelites from their enemies but before he was able to destroy the Philistines partly, he was stuck in life's experiences woven through a confusing tapestry of lack of focus, insatiable desires, and warped viewpoint of himself.

At a point in time, he was attacked by the Philistines because of his revenge on them and he killed them in thousands. Thereafter he was tired, exhausted, and got stuck with thirst. Instead of giving up and resigning to fate, he called out to God and God answered by not just providing cups of water but spring of water, which was named **En Hakore**, meaning "caller's spring" (Judges 13:15).

The law of confession teaches that there's a spring for every caller.

You're probably stuck in that situation because you've not called in faith, or that you called for an ungodly purpose (James 4:2-4), or perhaps you just haven't confessed positively enough (Jn 16:24).

HOLY TONGUE AND GOOD LIFE

The tongue that declares the words of liberty and turns misfortune to fortune must be free from deceit, lies and all forms of ungodliness. A tongue that is full of poison – wickedness, curses and negatives cannot confess and declare victories, success, and freedom from bondages.

Your prospect of love, life and good days is intricately linked with your confessions. "The one who wants to enjoy life and see good days [good—whether apparent or not], MUST KEEP HIS TONGUE FREE FROM EVIL AND HIS LIPS FROM SPEAKING GUILE (treachery, deceit). "HE MUST TURN AWAY FROM WICKEDNESS AND DO WHAT IS RIGHT. HE MUST SEARCH FOR PEACE [with god, with self, with others] AND PURSUE IT EAGERLY [actively—not merely desiring it]." (I Pet 3:10-11, AMP).

I agree with Dr. Tony Evans in one of his broadcasts on KHCB Radio when he said that God knew how deadly a tongue is - it's the only part of the body that is put behind bars. Your tongue and what comes out of it determine whether you get locked or unstuck. According to the Bible, ".. the tongue is a small part of the body, and yet it boasts of great things... the tongue is set among our members as that which contaminates the entire body, and sets on fire the course of our life [the cycle of man's existence], and is itself set on fire by hell..." (James 3:3-12 (AMP).

CONFESSING THE WORD THAT SETS FREE

This is a good place to conclude our discussions on the law of confession.

I must reemphasize that no single law in this book is stand-alone. As such, confession alone is not enough without the combination of other principles. David did not stop at the law of confession; he did more!

Jn 8:31-32 says, "Then said Jesus to those Jews which believed on him, If ye continue in my word, then are ye my disciples indeed; And ye shall know the truth, and the truth shall make you free."

God is the Word who transformed into human form that we call Jesus, the truth.

You can do many things with the Word, including obeying it, studying it, sharing it with others, and speaking it to address your situation. Job 22:28-29 says, "You will also decide and decree a thing, and it will be established for you; And the light [of God's favor] will shine upon your ways." (AMP).

Remember that your confession soon becomes your reality and that what you confess is what you possess. Your constant confessions are command buttons that shape or reshape your life.

God created a good world by good words, forming it by declaring, "...let there be light...", thus making a magnificent world from a formless world. The result was that "God looked over everything he had made; it was so good, so very good." (Gen 1:31, MSG).

When you're in a right standing with God, his word in your mouth is as powerful as his word in his mouth. So, keep saying what God's word is saying about your situation.

Create or recreate your world by confessing the truth of God's words.

Shape or reshape your life by saying good things to and about yourself always.

It shall be well with you! Amen!

13

GOD'S NAME DESTROYS FASTER THAN MISSILES

Understanding the Law of Identity

"Then said David to the Philistine, Thou comest to me with a sword, and with a spear, and with a shield: but I come to thee in the name of the Lord of hosts, the God of the armies of Israel, whom thou hast defied."
– I Sam 17:45

"For this reason also [because He obeyed and so completely humbled Himself], God has highly exalted Him and bestowed on Him the name which is above every name, so that at the name of Jesus every knee shall bow [in submission], of those who are in heaven and on earth and under the earth, and that every tongue will confess and openly acknowledge that Jesus Christ is Lord (sovereign God), to the glory of God the Father."
– Phil 2:9-11, AMP

"I will do anything you ask the Father in my name so that the Father will be given glory because of the Son."
– Jn 14:13, GW

"A name represents identity, a deep feeling and holds tremendous significance to its owner."

– Rachael Ingber

"Integrity: A name is the blueprint of the thing we call character. You ask, What's in a name? I answer, just about everything you do."

– Morris Mandel

221

NAME IS CRUCIAL

Name is a symbol of cultures, and reveals origin, preference, and tastes. It suggests intentions, moods, and modes. Name is crucial in all aspects of human lives because it speaks of the essence and identity of the bearer.

Jesus asked a demon-possessed man, "... "What is your name?" And he replied, "My name is Legion, because there are many of us inside this man." Then the evil spirits begged him again and again not to send them to some distant place." (Mk 5:8-10, NLT). This shows that every creature answers to a name whether they know their names and meanings or not.

God didn't complete the subprocess of creation until all creatures got their respective names, including all the animals and Adam's wife, Eve.

THE LAW OF IDENTITY

The law of identity states that *what you identify yourself with, either exposes you to danger or protects you; your identity then, is either an asset or a liability. Your name is your identity!*

God's name is His identity. Jesus Christ's name is His Identity. Everything, including virtues, blessings, honor, success, and victory, that God can ever give you is wrapped in His name. This is because His character, integrity, and ability are embedded in His name.

When you identify yourself with God's covenant name, you have a shelter of refuge to protect you from the twists, dangers, and oppressions of life.

"I AM WHO I AM"

God gave himself a name since no one existed before Him.

"I am the God of your ancestors, the God of Abraham, Isaac, and Jacob." ... Then Moses replied to God, "Suppose

I go to the people of Israel and say to them, 'The God of your ancestors has sent me to you,' and they ask me, 'What is his name?' What should I tell them?" God answered Moses, "I Am Who I Am. This is what you must say to the people of Israel: 'I am has sent me to you.' "Again God said to Moses, "This is what you must say to the people of Israel: The LORD God of your ancestors, the God of Abraham, Isaac, and Jacob, has sent me to you. This is my name forever. This is my title throughout every generation."

–Ex 3: 6, 13-15, GW

God is unique in all ways, some of which are his names.

- "God of Abraham, Isaac and Jacob"
- "I am Who I am"
- "I am".

And just to be sure, no need for an amendment: "This is my name forever". God sealed the deal with Moses and all the people.

Who else bears those names? Even when a person bears the same name throughout his lifetime (without nicknames) he becomes "the late" or "late Mr./Mrs. XWY" upon death! Not so with God who does not die.

Imagine you are on board in a plane, and your neighbor says, "hi! My name is Ron, nice to meet you", and you respond, "hi, nice meeting you too. My name is "I am"! What would your neighbor think or say?

Nobody bears "I am" because our uniqueness doesn't extend to bearing what God sets apart for himself.

The uniqueness of God's name stretches from eternity to eternity; it will continue to be efficacious without exceptions! When God said, "this is my name forever… my title throughout every generation" and three names attached to His (Abraham, Isaac, and Jacob), He tied His name to a covenant that He swore to those individuals, our patriarchs in the faith.

Recall that in I Samuel 17:43-44, Goliath had cursed David by his Philistine's god and threatened to feed the birds and wild animals with David's flesh. However, the reverse was the case because David countered him with "the name of the LORD **Almighty, the God of the armies of Israel**" whom Goliath had defied. (v. 45).

The name of the LORD Almighty which He handed down to the Patriarchs was a covenant guarantee under which David took refuge. When you operate in this guarantee, curses become empty and ineffective.

> ## As long as you call on God's name in righteousness, the blessings of that covenant flow to you.

In Exodus 3:12, God assured Moses, "I will be with you..." (GW). But before this time, He had related with Moses' forefathers as the God of Covenant.

- In Genesis 17:1, God promised Abraham, "...I am God Almighty. Live in my presence with integrity." God then went further, "You and your descendants in generations to come are to be faithful to my promise. This is how you are to be faithful to my promise: Every male among you is to be circumcised." (Gen 17:9-19, GW)

- In Genesis 26:3, God assured Isaac, "...I will be with you and bless you. I will give all these lands to you and your descendants. I will keep the oath that I swore to your father Abraham." (GW).

- In Gen 28:15-16, God assured Jacob, "Remember, I am with you and will watch over you wherever you go. I will also bring you back to this land because I will not leave you until I do what I've promised you." (GW).

By the reason of circumcision, every male child born to the Hebrews was part of the covenant heritage handed down from Abraham. Those outside of the Hebrews descent are part of this covenant with God by reason of their salvation in Christ Jesus. If you are in Christ Jesus, then you can activate the key to blessings in the Covenant.

David knew he was circumcised and belonged to the commonwealth of Israel. When Goliath trespassed with his mundane armor and maligned the name of God, David countered him with the very name of God which the giant had despised. That's why David defeated the giant. Proverbs 18:10 says, "The name of the LORD is a strong tower; the righteous runs to it and is safe and set on high [far above evil]." (AMP).

JESUS CHRIST'S NAME

Jesus' name was foretold by the angel: "She will give birth to a Son, and you shall name him Jesus (The LORD is salvation), for he will save his people from their sins." (Matt 1:21, AMP). His name was tied to his purpose, ability, and integrity. He was so named to eliminate devil's instrument of oppression (sin). His name was given to be above every other name (Phil 2:9) to demonstrate superiority over the hitherto existing names, including the names of the devil and his instruments.

After Balaam had attempted but unsuccessfully cursed the Israelites when hired by Balak, God opened the eyes of Balaam to see God's salvation plan for the Israelites, and by extension, for the world:

> "I see him, but not now; I behold him, but not near. A star will come out of Jacob; a scepter will rise out of Israel. He will crush the foreheads of Moab, the skulls of all the people of Sheth… his enemy will be conquered, but Israel will grow strong. A ruler will come out of Jacob."
>
> –Num 24:17-19, NIV

The star and ruler being referenced here is Jesus Christ whom God had ordained to destroy sin and all that it represents such as the oppression that Goliath brought against the Israelites and the obstacles that devil brings your way.

David countered Goliath with the name of the Lord and got victory. Your own oppressor might have come against you in the form of bad health, bad debt, failure in life, ministry and business, bad marriage and looming foreclosure of assets. Whatever! Launch your counterattack with the name of Jesus Christ, the most potent tool in your kitty.

All the knees of oppression must bow.

THE INTEGRITY OF HIS NAME

Talking about the excellency of His name, the Bible says, "having become as much superior to angels, since He has inherited a more excellent *and* glorious name than they [that is, Son—the name above all names]" (Heb 1:4, AMP).

So, God's covenant name that wrought victory for David, is the same name Jesus inherited, to save the world. God's name is Jesus's identity!

When you call on His covenant (holy) name, you appeal to His integrity which doesn't fail; you ask Him to let you experience who He is and what He can do in your circumstances. The Bible says, "…You can count on it. From now on, whatever you request along the lines of who I am and what I am doing, I'll do it. That's how the Father will be seen for who he is in the Son. I mean it. Whatever you request in this way, I'll do." (Jn 14:13-14, MSG).

> "I AM WHO I AM" among other things, means "I am the LORD, I do not change…" (Mal 3:6)

I imagine God in that scripture saying: *call me my name anytime, for anything I have ever promised, I will respond. If you ever called me for anything before and I answered, I will answer yet again because the same integrity that I had in the past, is still the same that I have now and would be the same I will ever have. I do not change. I do not grow older nor do I diminish in age or person. I do not get better; I have no improvement because nothing else could be better outside of me…"*

"BECAUSE HE KNOWS MY NAME…"

Though Psalm 91 is generally regarded as prayers of God's protection, it's more than that. They are prayers that draw on all the possibilities of God, including victory over all manners of shackles that God's children may be enmeshed in – death, disaster, shame, storms, pestilence, and many more.

Happily, the chapter is replete with different kinds of recipes and panaceas, all of which work like weapons to discomfit and triumph over oppressions. One of them is stated in verse fourteen: *God's name.*

> "… I will set him [securely] on high, because he knows My name [he confidently trusts and relies on Me, knowing I will never abandon him, no, never]. "He will call upon Me, and I will answer him; I will be with him in trouble; I will rescue him and honor him."
>
> –Ps 91:14-15, AMP

But before God's name could get you unshackled, you must acknowledge it. This means that you must recognize it with explicit confidence that it's the final authority over your tempest. Acknowledging God's name includes calling on it for help, out of a pure heart and for just reasons.

GOD'S NAME FOLLOWS YOU AND FIGHTS FOR YOU

Jesus had given the seventy-two disciples power over Satan who fell like lightening before them during their evangelistic exploits. Jesus knew that His gospel was a natural repellant to Satan and that he (Satan) would stop at nothing to fight back just as in fact he would fight against your quest for freedom from his oppression.

> "The seventy-two men came back in great joy. "Lord," they said, "even the demons obeyed us when we gave them a command in your name!" Jesus answered them, "I saw Satan fall like lightning from heaven. Listen! I have given you authority, so that you can walk on snakes and scorpions and overcome all the power of the Enemy, and nothing will hurt you."
>
> –Lk 10:17-20, GNT

As a true child of God, when your steps are ordered by God in certain directions, He would go ahead of you to procure the routes for your safety and texture the grounds for your success. He'd tie down principalities that are poised to hold you down. That is what God did for David when he approached Goliath with the name of God - the covenant power of God.

The greatness of God's power is manifested in his awesome presence, especially in response to the call of his name in his honor. Upon manifestation, the enemies cringe and fear in submission to his name which is above theirs. The Bible says, "All the nations surrounded me, but armed with the name of the LORD, I defeated them." (Ps 118:10, GW).

The seventy-two disciples reported that demons submitted to them in Jesus' name (See Luke 10:17). Why would evil spirits bow to a name? It's the name of Jesus (the authority He had given them) that made demons to bow down in subjection. (See verse 19).

> The amazing result was that as demons were quaking and bowing down in subjection to the name of Jesus, chains were falling off victims' hands, problems were being solved, and poor people were rejoicing at the good news of Jesus. As all these were happening, the seventy-two evangelists were getting unstuck and fulfilling their mission purpose. Amen! Alleluias!

Jesus always foots the bill of his orders; he owes no man. When he gives you a vision, he makes provisions for its accomplishment. One of such provisions is the covenant heritage and power of his name (see John 14:13). It's the recognition and honor attached to his name that crushed Satan at their feet. (See Philippians 2:9).

The name of God carries God's presence:

"Long ago when the Israelis escaped from Egypt, from that land of foreign tongue, then the lands of Judah and of Israel became God's new home and kingdom. The Red Sea saw them coming and quickly broke apart before them. The Jordan River opened up a path for them to cross. The mountains skipped like rams, the little hills like lambs! What's wrong, Red Sea, that made you cut yourself in two? What happened, Jordan River, to your waters? Why were they held back? Why, mountains, did you skip like rams? Why, little hills, like lambs? Tremble, O earth, at the presence of the Lord, the God of Jacob. For he caused gushing streams to burst from flinty rock."

–Ps 114:1-7, TLB

The wonder of God's covenant name is in his glorious presence which unmistakably guarantees victories for those living right with God. The "Lord of Jacob" in verse 7 is a remarkable appellation which references God's covenant with Jacob, who together with Isaac, were Abraham's direct covenant descendants.

God had assured Jacob, "Remember, I am with you and will watch over you wherever you go. I will also bring you back to this land because I will not leave you until I do what I've promised you." (Gen 28:15-16, GW). Thus, the invocation of the Lord of Jacob means the omniscient God would honor his promise to be with those who call on his covenant name.

The Israelites were on a mission to serve God and prosper in the promise land (of Canaan), having been delivered from Pharaoh's bondage by God's mighty hands and terrible acts of righteousness. The "mountains", "hills", "Jordan", "seas", collectively, literally, and figuratively represent obstacles to prevent them from enjoying their covenant redemptive blessings. Think of Ai, Jericho, Amalekites, and Philistines. These were progress resisters.

God's presence is not limited to one location. As his presence was inspiring David and bringing out his needed skills, the same presence was uncovering Goliath's *Achilles heels* - his uncovered eye that hosted David's flaming brutal stone.

Goliath's inner eyes were blinded because he couldn't realize that it was a suicide mission to "defy the name of...God". And now, his physical eyes are gone. What is left of a man whose physical and spiritual eyes are no more except to stumble and wobble into extinction and become "food to the birds of the air"? Thanks to the redemptive power of God's name!

Your problems are no exceptions to the extinguishing power of God's presence when you call on his name and totally depend on him for solution. Your *giant* may appear to be an indomitable champion of repute but God's presence will mark it down for extinction.

Keep calling his name. Keep trusting him. And keep hoping for the best.

He HEARS when you call his name, for he's not deaf.

He SPEAKS when you cry unto his name because He's not dumb.

He MOVES in His majestic and awesome presence when you invoke His covenant name for solutions. He's not immobilized stuck-to-one-place or portable Dagon of the Philistines.

He is omnipresent and not a zombie! He will come at the nick of time!

God's presence may appear unseen; it is felt, nonetheless.

The pain and illness might still be there, however, like he inspired David while Goliath was still boasting, He'll inspire the physicians to improve their skills toward the next surgery (which doesn't have to take place anyway). He'd inspire scientists to discover new medicines or vaccines toward the next solutions to your ailment.

As he's inspiring health workers, he may choose to address your Goliath directly by making it disappear - instant healing and disappearance of illnesses. Miracles still happen. He's God of miracles and is not limited by your problems.

Perhaps your obstacles are not health related. Whatever they are, God can still inspire you for solutions even as he's working out their elimination.

David's confidence in God's name was strong. He had said, "The LORD hear thee in the day of trouble; the name of the God of Jacob defend thee…" (Ps 20:1). And, after His victory over Goliath, King Saul was after his life because of jealousy. David prayed to God, "Save me, O God, by Your name…." (Ps. 54:1). He was saved!

Call His nam e today.

14

"VERB IS A 'DOING WORD'"

Practicing the Law of Action

"As the Philistine moved closer to attack him, David ran quickly toward the battle line to meet him. Reaching into his bag and taking out a stone, he slung it and struck the Philistine on the forehead. The stone sank into his forehead, and he fell facedown on the ground.

So David triumphed over the Philistine with a sling and a stone; without a sword in his hand he struck down the Philistine and killed him.

David ran and stood over him. He took hold of the Philistine's sword and drew it from the sheath. After he killed him, he cut off his head with the sword."

- I Sam 17:48-51, NIV

"It is not the critic who counts; not the man who points out how the strong man stumbles or where the doer of deeds could have done better. The credit belongs to the man who is actually in the arena, whose face is marred by dust and sweat and blood, who strives valiantly, who errs and comes up short again and again, because there is no effort without error or shortcoming, but who knows the great enthusiasms, the great devotions, who spends himself for a worthy cause; who, at the best, knows, in the end, the triumph of high achievement, and who, at the worst, if he fails, at least he fails while daring greatly, so that his place shall never be with those cold and timid souls who knew neither victory nor defeat."

- Theodore Roosevelt

I like soccer game not only because of its interesting twists and turns but also because of sundry lessons that come with it. During the life of a game, we have seen winning sides eventually lose, and losing sides come from the rear to win the league title.

That was the experience in the match between Ashton Villa FC (AVL) and Liverpool in the 2020/2021 European Premiership League (EPL) season.

Liverpool were the defending champion having clinched the title in the 2019/2020 edition. Even though AVL were the winning side, they were still dogged, up and doing to maintain their lead. The Liverpool players were also relentless in their efforts to reduce the tally, at least. However, the harder they tried, the wider their loss margin.

The AVL-Liverpool game leaves one with many lessons, one of which is this: *don't just top the list, multiply your lead such that the more your opponent seeks to catch up on you, the farther you are in victory.* This is important because anything can happen. The underdog may turn into a champion and displace your lead.

We are all AVL as well as Liverpool in that game at different times in our lives. We've had the title of a champion in some areas but sometimes, things happen along the way, and we have our titles shamefully challenged especially from unlikely sources and find it pretty difficult to catch up. We get stuck. We are dazed, shaken and shackled.

David stayed through till he killed Goliath.

Like the AVL team, we too may have been confined to or emerge from a near-relegation past due to factors beyond our control. But we have control over our choices now and we can choose not to allow our past determine our future. We have the choice to improve on our *Achilles heels*. We have all it takes to challenge *the champion* - whatever it is that poses as our *status quo*.

In your efforts to win victory, don't just win and let down your guards; multiply your lead. Maintain your lead till the end of your life. The world is full of "exs" - ex-millionaires, ex-presidents, ex-governors, ex-CEOs, etcetera, etcetera. If you must be an "ex", then it should not be an ex-winner or an ex-successful person.

The game of AVL vs Liverpool ended 7:2 in favor of AVL, thus breaking a record of over fifty years when the last defending champion faced such a defeat.

Did you realize that the scoreboard was clean (0-0) at the first kick of the ball? What replaced "0" besides their names was what they did or didn't do in the course of the game, which in this case included tact, substitutions, communication, right application of known principles, knowledge of opponents' strength and weaknesses, directed efforts, synergy, and team spirit.

What will eventually replace the blank space between your Date of Birth and Date of Death are your competitive advantages and productive actions taken in furtherance of your goals.

Welcome to life, things happen here. But one thing that you must never allow to happen is to give up. You must keep fighting until you win.

David *ran* quickly toward the battle line to meet Goliath.

THE LAW OF ACTION

The law of action states that, ***action is the mother of events; momentous, timely and targeted action is the wing of thoughts and planning; therefore, act decisively.*** The beauty of the law of action is in its focus, coordination, and predictability.

After you have drawn a mental conclusion of success and victory by faith, you then act swiftly. Mere actions are not enough to break your shackles, for if it were, everyone in motion would have been self-made success.

To break limits, you must act discreetly, timely, purposely, and momentously. You must not just "go" but "go to get there." It is good to act, but it's the best to act decisively.

Scalar and vector

Scalars are quantities that have only magnitude (size or numerical value) whereas vectors are quantities that have both a magnitude and a direction. Scalars' quantities are measured by distance, speed, time, power, and energy. Vectors' quantities change where there is change in magnitude and directions.

Many people are like Scalars – they measure what they are supposed to get out of life by their sizes (basically their physical qualities or by the numbers of their age). *"I am in my 40s, all of these damn setbacks shouldn't happen to me." "I am good looking handsome guy, why am I still having relationship problems?" "People always tell me that I am cute and beautiful; how come I don't have stable relationships?"*

Like scalars, some people measure their lives by efforts they have put into life in terms of distance, speed, power, and energy. Unfortunately, this is not so with God, because "... No one shall succeed by strength alone." (I Sam 2:9, TLB)

Getting meaningful results out of life requires not just moving with magnitude but also with clear direction, like vectors quantities. You must consciously draw a target and work out a propitious time to strike. David ran toward Goliath – he moved with magnitude and direction.

Most of the times, we're the one impeding God by our inactions or wrong actions. We are reluctant to act because we're expecting a perfect condition which may never come. The Bible says, "If you wait for perfect conditions, you will never get anything done." (Eccl 11:4, TLB) (See Proverbs 6:10-19; 23:33-34).

UP AND DOING

Henry Wadsworth Longfellow, in his famous poem, *"A Psalm of Life"*, concluded with a tone of encouragement to act and wait in hope. But before then, we understand his argument that our actions and their consequences survive us because they are not what God commanded to return to dust. Longfellow argued, and I agree, that, life is real, and that grave is not its end.

Longfellow was compelling in his words, "… Act, – act in the living Present! Heart within, and God o'erhead!" He went on:

Lives of great men all remind us
We can make our lives sublime,
And, departing, leave behind us

Footprints on the sands of time;
Footprints, that perhaps another,
 Sailing o'er life's solemn main,
A forlorn and shipwrecked brother,
Seeing, shall take heart again.

Let us, then, be up and doing,
With a heart for any fate;
Still achieving, still pursuing,
Learn to labor and to wait.[1]

You must put God's promises, instructions, and directions in perspective and into action, lest they remain only "spiritual blessings". Some of the "actions" may be praying fervently before your problems could go away, or to network, connect, synergize, or advertise. It may even be to go back to school, or learn a new trade, or get additional trainings in your discipline.

If you took a quick count of the *active verbs* in I Samuel 17:48-51 (*King James Version*), you'd discover *fifteen* active verbs describing David's immediate actions that killed Goliath.

- **v. 48 - David <u>hastened</u>**

David was proactively active. He did not wait till Goliath overtook him but moved swiftly to "take the bull by the horn."

"Goliath arose and came" to attack David just as spiritual attacks, bad health, and financial crisis invade to make us miserable or kill us. Goliath invaded David just as bad addictions, bad relationships, poor career choices and other social vices catch up on us unawares to impoverish us.

Like David, we must proactively 'hasten" and not wait for perfect conditions before swinging into actions. Proverbs 21:25 says "Lazy people finally die of hunger because they won't get up and go to work." (MESSAGE)

- **v. 48 - <u>ran</u> toward**

You need to be like *vectors quantities* which do not only have magnitude but also direction. ***Magnitude without direction would land you anywhere! The people who go "anywhere" would find themselves "anywhere" and that's a good description for wandering.*** It's hard, if not impossible, to conceive a successful person who is a wanderer. Certainly, "anywhere" and "everywhere" are no clear destinations.

> David ran toward Goliath; he did not beat about the bush. As you move toward your goal in life, be resolute that you are not just moving but moving toward your goal. There is usually no reward for a race without mark!

- **v. 49 -** <u>put</u> his hand in his bag

There is no one who's without what to work with.

David' bag contained stones and arrows – the weapons. You must arm yourself mentally and materially to get unstuck from whatever that is holding you down. The contents of your own "bag" might be improved skills, intellectual abilities, or even material possessions. What's important is to be armed with weapons necessary and meant to fight a battle that is particular to you.

- v. 49 - <u>took</u> thence a stone
- v. 49 - <u>slang</u> it
- v. 49 - <u>smote</u> the Philistine in his forehead

The combinations of the above three actions words – "took thence a stone", "slang it", "smote the Philistine in his forehead" demonstrate the utmost use of David's skills.

The Bible says that "Diligent hands will rule, but laziness ends in forced labor." (Prov 12:24, NIV). You must be sure to have your weapon ready for use, at any time.

It is not enough to act, just as it's not enough to merely deploy your weapons. You must skillfully maneuver them to put you in the lead. *Your inability to skillfully fight with your weapons can make you a victim of your own sword.*

Stay through till you win

Nothing ventured; nothing won! The summary of the rest *(nine)* of David's actions in verses 50 and 51 is two words – consistency and persistence.

- v. 50 - <u>prevailed</u> over the Philistine
- v. 50 - <u>smote</u> the Philistine
- v. 50 - <u>slew</u> him
- v. 51 - David <u>ran</u>
- v. 51 - <u>Stood</u> upon the Philistine

- v. 51 - <u>took</u> his sword
- v.51 - <u>drew</u> it out of the sheath thereof
- v.51 - <u>slew</u> him
- v.51 - <u>cut</u> off his head therewith

You must act, continue to act, and consummate your actions with a victory experience.

David did not stop half-way; he was focused and committed to getting out the odds called Goliath. Likewise, you must stay focused on victory and avoid distractions.

> You want to avoid mediocrity like a plague; past victories, present success and comforts may be enemies of future victories. Know where to draw the line.

It's not enough to have knowledge. Knowledge is relative and limited; and the limit of your knowledge is the extent of your actions. You must complement your knowledge with momentous and decisive actions. The knowledge of your entitlements or inheritance automatically places you in a great advantage but the practical steps you make in furtherance of its reality puts you in greater advantage.

Learn from the athletes. However fast they ran in the middle of the race, it's the first three to breast the tape that receive trophies. *Breasting the tape connotes the end of the race. Your race to get unstuck doesn't end until you sever the monster's head and take the plunders. If your Goliath's head is still on his neck, then you are as precarious as sleeping in the lions' den.*

In battle lines, all the soldiers do the fighting but the victors are the ones who are alive and take the plunders. Victories without plunders are wanderings and pyrrhic victories. "Plunders" in this sense connote significant evidence of overpowering of the vanquished.

David did not stop fighting until he severed Goliath's head from his body. Likewise, don't stop fighting your bad health, bad addictions, social dysfunctions, current trends toward financial wreck and looming marriage fiasco.

Don't stop until you win.

PRINCIPLES OF THE LAW OF ACTION

Let's consider some of the principles of the law of action.

DIVINE DIRECTION

It's of no use running at the peak of your speed if you are heading a wrong way! Don't be a scalar whose quantity has only magnitude; be a vector quantity that has both magnitude and direction.

The surest path to good success is divine direction. Neither success nor victory is certain in the absence of divine direction. Peter and his colleagues had worked hard – they had taken resolute actions to succeed. Unfortunately, life was not ready to give them what they had labored hard to acquire – fishes.

Like most of us, Peter and company did what they knew how to do but they were stuck with failures. But Jesus showed up and gave them direction. "Take the boat into deep water, and lower your nets to catch some fish." The results? "...they caught a great number of fish, and their net was breaking" (Lk 5:6, NKJV).

ACT WITH PURPOSE (ACT TO WIN)

The Apostle Paul was stoned. Shipwrecked. Provoked. Persecuted. Flogged brutally. Misunderstood. Mocked. Attacked. Harassed. How did he survive? He ran straight to the goal with purpose in every step. He fought to win.

> "In a race everyone runs, but only one person gets first prize. So run your race to win. To win the contest you must

deny yourselves many things that would keep you from doing your best... So I run straight to the goal with purpose in every step. I fight to win. I'm not just shadow-boxing or playing around. Like an athlete I punish my body, treating it roughly, training it to do what it should, not what it wants to. Otherwise I fear that after enlisting others for the race, I myself might be declared unfit and ordered to stand aside."

- I Cor 9:24-27, TLB

Like David, Apostle Paul ran "straight to the goal with purpose in every step." He fought to win.

MOVE TOWARD THE TARGET

David ran toward Goliath. He had done enough of permutations, drawn enough conclusions of victory in his mind, and imagined victory already. He then swiftly moved toward the target. "As the Philistine moved closer to attack him, David ran quickly toward the battle line to meet him…" (I Sam 17:48). The direction of Goliath mattered to him.

If you are into business, you must "situate" in the direction of "human traffic." In other words, conduct your business in an area where your business items are needed. You must never sell products that nobody would want to buy. Let your business drive values that people would get in exchange of money.

From the first day of your business' financial year, ensure that all activities and programs run toward the year's goals. Make sure all resources, trainings, budgets, and transactions are in the direction of the corporate goals as you determine that nothing is wasted.

DISCIPLINE YOUR BODY

Your body system consists of all your organs and how they relate to ensure you have good health. This includes your physique, carriage and countenance which all have direct bearings on your purpose in life. Your body is given by God to relate with the terrestrial just as your spirit is to the supernatural. The healthier you are, the more likely you are to get good things done. This underscores the importance of a healthy living.

Your sound health is a good factor that determines your actions, reactions, keeping appointments, studying, networking, and especially, the relationships that you keep. If you're healthy, you'll most likely have healthy relationships.

By design, your body system relates to one another; and weakness to one is weakness to all.

> Those who are "going to get to" their purposes with success in mind would carry and use their bodies carefully.

Avoid unnecessary self-indulgence. Make discipline a *sine qua non*. Effective body discipline includes training and taming by denying it excesses and rationing all that it wants.

BREAK YOUR FALLOW GROUND

Hos 10:12-13 says, "Sow to yourselves in righteousness, reap in mercy; break up your fallow ground: for it is time to seek the LORD, till he come and rain righteousness upon you..."

A fallow ground is a land which has been left uncultivated for a long time and has become outgrown with weeds and thorns, and now possibly become infested with animals and rodents.

It is believed that fallow grounds are rich in requisite mineral contents that now serve as fertilizer upon cultivation and seed planting. It is imperative to break your fallow ground because you must not waste useful resources for lack of cultivation.

Successful people don't waste useful resources. Breaking your fallow ground connotes breaking from inertia because a farmer who failed to plant in season will have no crop to harvest.

Your experiences, untapped strength, uncultivated gifts and talents, undeveloped skills and dreams and desires that you have done nothing about are typical illustrations of your fallow ground. You must cultivate those grounds before you could gather harvests from them.

ACT WITH ENTHUSIASM

Samuel Ullman said, "Nobody grows old merely by living a number of years. We grow old by deserting our ideals. Years may wrinkle the skin, but to give up enthusiasm wrinkles the soul."

The word enthusiasm comes from Greek word "entheos" which translates to being possessed of god or literally, "god within". It describes words such as intense, interest or enjoyment or a sort of passion aroused by inspiration within.

When enthusiasm meets with relevant skills, your success becomes measurable and predictable. When this happens, your heart beats differently - not "hyperly" or "tensely". As you know, success is not too far from a healthy person.

When passion dies in a man, mediocrity sets in, and complaints, blame game, apathy, and vagaries become inevitable. He suddenly becomes defensive and negative in his attitudes. As you probably know, a man with enthusiasm is greater than a hundred with mere wishes!

CONTEST OR CONTEND

The inhabitants of Canaan that the Israelites failed to dislodge became problems to them. God had warned them in advance to drive out the inhabitant otherwise "…those which ye let remain of them shall be pricks in your eyes, and thorns in your sides, and shall vex you in the land wherein ye dwell." (Num 33:55).

The Israelites failed to grow to capacity; they were unsuitable specimens in God's hands during the trial process. For example, I Chronicles 9:1 says, "… And Judah was carried away into exile to Babylon because of their unfaithfulness [to God]." (AMP).

Therefore you must contend in prayers and other actions to enjoy your inheritance in Chris Jesus.

Some of the Israelites tribes could not enjoy their inheritance because they could not contest with the inhabitants. So, they had to be content with sharing their possessions involuntarily (See Joshua 15:63; 17:12-13).

ACT WITH HOPES AND EXPECTATIONS

David ran toward Goliath with hope that Goliath would be dead. He did not doubt God's ability or the effectiveness of his proven weapons in his bag. He had positive expectations.

Prophet Elijah got the whole nation of Israel unstuck by persistent prayers. Seven times Elijah asked his servant to check out the skies whether clouds had gathered (I Kgs 18:41-46).

Elijah did not just pray; he prayed expectantly.

Between the first bending of his knees in prayers and the eventual heavy downpours lay the warm fervor of passion, faith and confidence which moved the invisible hands of the Almighty God to release the rain.

> Prayers, the avowed best synergy to ever exist, and the inestimable core principle of the law of action, must be offered in hope and expectations or they become a mere exercise of pointless routine drudgery.

FAITH IN ACTION

Risk is the effect of uncertainty over your goals and objectives. That's why you or your organization must make efforts to mitigate different types of risks, ranging from personal to business and corporate.

Scripturally, actions based on faith in God's words are faith in action. Other people might want to call this a *risk*. But when risk is divorced from faith in God or in His word, it's mere "trying out some guess work or some luck game".

Merely taking a risk means you don't really believe that you would succeed but that you just want to "do something, who knows?" But taking a risk by taking a step (or leap) of faith happens because you believe that it's worthwhile, God-directed, and therefore, you would succeed.

In Numbers chapter thirteen, we see faith in action in the account of the spies who went to spy the land of Canaan.

The "spies" were "risk takers" who were on an expedition to chart the parts unknown, discover the hidden, and take knowledge from the unknown. Their actions were faith-based because they moved on the heels of God-inspired directions from their leader.

> It's not that achieving greatness in life is difficult for many of us. It's because many of us are unwilling to take necessary risks in life.

Only Caleb and Joshua were willing, ready, and able to take faith-actions (Numbers 13:39). They got the rewards of their faith (Numbers 14:30). Many spies were given the same opportunity to make history but only two people were risk takers. The majority that was timid did not enter the promise land.

You don't have to have or master all the facts, neither should you have all the knowledge. It's enough to know something about the subject matter, including knowing that God is involved in the task - that God has spoken and that He would do it even though it doesn't look like it.

God called Abram and told him to get out of his country, his people and his father's land, "to a land I will shew thee." (Gen 12:1). Not having known all the facts, detailed itinerary, or proof of a secured future, Abram set out without objections. Wasn't that a risk? Absolutely! A risk in action; yes, faith in action! All he needed to "have" and "know" is "God said...".

Taking faith-based risks is part of your fundamental "must-haves" in your quest to get unstuck.

I believe these words below on risk taking will inspire you.

> To laugh is to risk appearing a fool,
> To weep is to risk appearing sentimental.
> To reach out to another is to risk involvement,
> To expose feelings is to risk exposing your true self.

To place your ideas and dreams before a crowd is to risk their loss.
To love is to risk not being loved in return,
To live is to risk dying,
To hope is to risk despair,
To try is to risk failure.
But risks must be taken because the greatest hazard in life is to risk nothing.
The person who risks nothing, does nothing, has nothing, is nothing.
He may avoid suffering and sorrow,
But he cannot learn, feel, change, grow or live.
Chained by his servitude he is a slave who has forfeited all freedom.
Only a person who risks is free."[2]

I am sure you know that criminal actions are bad risks! In the context of our discourse on "action" or law of action, we limit our expression of risks to taking actions despite uncertainties because we know that God is involved – God is with us.

ELIMINATE FEAR

Don't settle where fear puts you. Fear either stagnates you or makes you retreat. Either way, that's not a way to "have good success."

> **Fear naturally emanates from a confused mind because confusions, uncertainties and fears are companions.**

Sometimes fear is not entirely bad. It's what you do while fearful that determines whether the outcome would be bad. You must overcome your fear with assurances of God's promises.

Under the law of identity, we talked about the abiding presence of God embedded in His name. "God has not given us the spirit of fear but of power, love and sound mind." (II Tim 1:7). *Through sound mind, the wisdom of God would guide you to make sound and productive decisions.*

DON'T JUST ASK: "WHAT IF I FAIL?" BUT ALSO ASK "WHAT IF I SUCCEED?"

The fact is that eventually, you really do not lose pretty much, if at all, when you fail in your first attempts. It's when you stop trying that you become a failure. Failure is an event and not final until you call it so. We have seen and heard of great people who once failed.

The Wright Brothers, Wilbur and Orville had conducted failed experiments before their historic first flight. One of the earlier failures was when they flipped a coin to decide who would fly first. Wilbur won the coin toss but he over-steered with the elevator after leaving the launching rail. The flyer climbed too steeply, stalled, and later landed on the sand. It had failed. A couple of days later on December 17, 1903, it was Orville's turn. He had learnt from Wilbur's earlier mistakes and improved on the techniques. Orville succeeded.

"Again, the flyer was unruly, pitching up and down as Orville overcompensated with the controls. But he kept it aloft until it hit the sand about 120 feet from the rail. Into the 27-mph wind, the groundspeed had been 6.8 mph, for a total airspeed of 34 mph... Wilbur's second flight - the fourth and last of the day — was an impressive 852 feet in 59 seconds."[3]

You want to be like Edmund Hillary, Abraham Lincoln, Albert Einstein, who all failed in their initial attempts to solve human problems but eventually succeeded.

MINIMIZE THE SIZE OF YOUR ORDEALS, MAGNIFY OPPORTUNITIES

In their focused, forward-looking, *risky* actions, successful people focus on reaching their goals rather than magnifying their distractions.

Paul minimized his terrible ordeals as "light affliction" compared to the "eternal weight glory" that awaited him (II Cor 4:16-18). Joshua and Caleb swung into *risk-in-action* voyage, minimized the towering sizes of the descendants of the Anakites because they believed Hebron was meant to be their inheritance. They got it! (Joshua 14).

You'll be surprised to realize that the greater percentage of your fears would not happen.

DETERMINATION STRONGER THAN DEATH

Excelling determination is premised on God's promises, anchored on his love, strengthened by his words, and guided by his Holy Spirit. It's not borne out of mere egoistic, self-serving pursuit of materialistic gains.

Your determination to succeed at all costs in the face of daunting challenges must not just stem from mere mental assent but based on a KNOWING- an inward persuasion that reinforces unflinching conviction and edged on confidence that you "can do all things through Christ who strengthens you." (Phil 4:13).

According to Paul when he said, "Who shall ever separate us from the love of Christ? Will tribulation, or distress, or persecution, or famine, or nakedness, or danger, or sword?... For I am convinced [and continue to be convinced—beyond any doubt] that neither death, nor life, nor angels, nor principalities, nor things present *and* threatening, nor things to come, nor powers, nor height, nor depth, nor any other created thing, will be able to separate us from the [unlimited] love of God, which is in Christ Jesus our Lord. (Rom 8:35-39, AMP).

The determination that wins says *I know I'm pursuing God's plan for my life under His direction and to this extent, God's got my back. He will not let me fail...*"

SUMMING IT UP - ACT NOW

Several months after qualifying as an attorney in Nigeria, I applied in response to a national advert by ExxonMobil for trainee legal counsel, but it seemed I was going to wait forever.

I could no longer wait in the world of emails and phone calls. Armed with copies of my resume, one day I set out, starting from the uptown commercial areas of Lagos where there were many law offices. I had determined not to go back home until all copies of my resume were personally distributed and contacts collected for follow ups.

I had prayed, strategized, and got enough of theoretical guidance on how to get jobs. Now I had to *jump into the volcano*. Meanwhile, I had enrolled for my graduate program in law at my alma mater, Obafemi Awolowo University, Nigeria, expecting to start course work in the next spring. Because I didn't want to tamper with the little savings that I had kept for my graduate courses, I determined to walk to anywhere my legs could carry me.

By the way, ExxonMobil job interview was later scheduled to hold on a date that coincided with my final graduate exam- energy and natural resources law exam. I emailed them for a reschedule. Maybe I'd hear back from them tomorrow.

At about midday, I found Chief B. O. Benson (SAN) Law Offices. As part of the legal traditions inherited from the British legal system, we have the privileged body of practicing lawyers who are conferred with the status of the Senior Advocate of Nigeria (SAN) based on their distinctions in the practice of law and/or significant intellectual contributions to the development of law and practice.

Their privilege includes having their cases called out of turn while in court to save their time. It is a privilege that comes with a great influence not only in the legal profession but also in the larger society. Some of them who are locally recognized by their local communities with chieftaincy titles prefer to go by "Chief" stating their names to read, *"Chief John Doe (SAN).*

The owner of this law office, Chief Benson, is one of such privileged lawyers. He was admitted into the English Bar in 1959 and into Nigeria Bar the same year. He was formerly the General Secretary and later the President of the Nigerian Bar Association.

So, I walked in, introduced myself and was asked to see the then Managing Partner. After a brief interview, I was asked when I could start working. My answer was sharp: "immediately, now!" The Managing Partner laughed out loud but later controlled himself and apologized for laughing out loud. "Oh, I'm sorry for that Mr. Adepoju....". Then he cleared his throat and resumed, "...well, well, we are extremely impressed by your resume and your performance at the interview. We don't mind hiring you 'immediately, now' (gesticulating to put 'immediately, now' in inverted comma) but we've got to put certain things in place for you. You can start on Monday."

That's the end. The rest is history.

I never lost a case in court throughout my work with Chief B. O. Benson (SAN) Law Offices or anywhere I ever worked. No doubt, I was a bright dynamic "green wig", (as they called new lawyers in those days) with impressive resume and "yes I can" attitude (and still I possess these qualities).

I had networked with high profile people, including Justices of the Court of Appeal, Bar leaders and a few SANs, having been an active literary and debating team member, moot and mock trial member, and a member of the *Equity Chambers* of the Law Faculty of the Obafemi Awolowo University, and later, the President of the Christian Law Students Fellowship of Nigeria (CLASFON) at the Nigerian Law School.

But as important as being a bright new wig and my networking skills, they could not substitute for the overarching importance of focused, target and momentum actions that eventually brought my first dream job as a new wig.

Remember that the law of action states in part that, *action is the mother of events; momentous, timely and targeted action is the wing of thoughts and planning; therefore, act decisively.* Remember also that you must not act like scalars that have only the magnitude; you must be like vectors quantities that possess both magnitude and direction.

Do not just act or measure your life by *distance you've made in life (activities), or by your size (financial weight or otherwise), or by length of time (age or years of doing a thing); in addition to all of these, act with direction (with a target, goal, objective, or clear mission).*

I am resolute in this, that the world would be much better than this if everyone would think as though there's no obstacle, act as though there's no fear, and win as though there's no failure. Whoever has conquered fear, has conquered life itself, for victory over fear is victory over failure, defeats, and mediocrity.

David killed Goliath not because he merely acted but because he acted with purpose and precision. He ran toward him– he did not go for the sake of movement, he advanced on a mission to kill Goliath.

Take that timeous and decisive step now with magnitude and direction. You will have victory in Jesus' name.

15

THE SUPERNATURAL CONTROLS THE NATURAL

Marshalling the Weapons of Warfare

EVERY PROBLEM HAS SPIRITUAL ROOTS

Your problematic experiences are the offshoots of certain spiritual problems. When the spiritual problems are unresolved, each corresponding effort in the natural realm would be counterproductive. It's therefore important to address and overcome problems first in the spiritual realm.

Before David confronted Goliath, he had both hands-on and spiritual trainings. He once praised God for having trained his hands for battles and taught him how to bend a bow. (Ps 144:1).

MARSHALLING THE WEAPONS OF WARFARE

So, instead of asking whether there'll be spiritual warfare or battles, it's wise to ask yourself how prepared you are.

As you've learned in this book, there's no single, exclusive principle that gives ultimate victory because David used many principles that culminated in his victory over Goliath. You might have practiced some of the principles of success and still get stuck. Have you considered spiritual weapons? Where did you start your work from - physical or spiritual realm?

Spiritual warfare is a war that goes in the spirit realm but which consequences you feel or experience physically or emotionally. It's a battle between the light and darkness, principally orchestrated by devil against God's children. As one with right standing with God, you're fighting the devil and his agents not for victory but from a victory point because the devil is a defeated foe already. You only need to work with God.

Devil, the thief, keeps stealing and destroying people's lives with his spiritual weapons. It's therefore important to be careful "because your adversary the devil, as a roaring lion, walketh about, seeking whom he may devour." (I Pet 5:8).

Ephesians 6:10-19 explains the weapons of our (spiritual) warfare.

Let's discuss this portion of the Bible in context, briefly and systemically.

...BE STRONG IN THE LORD, AND IN THE POWER OF HIS MIGHT

You can have many sources where you tap your power, strength, and motivation – friends, parents, money, national military and some sort of fighting skills. You may even get your spiritual strength from the lesser gods.

To get truly unstuck however, you've got to be strong in the Lord and his mighty power. In other words, you must leverage on God's power (God's word) for strength. Apostle Paul stated that he was not ashamed of the gospel of Christ because it is the power of God for the salvation (Rom 1:16).

When the enemies raided David's camp and took away his family members, he was distressed but he "...found strength in the LORD his God." (I Sam 30:6, GW). David was able to overcome his obstacles because he was strong in the Lord. He also said, "My soul finds rest in God alone; my salvation comes from him." (Ps 62:1).

Wait on God and He would renew your strength. Isaiah 40:31 assures, "But they that wait upon the LORD **shall renew their strength; they shall mount up with wings as eagles; they shall run, and not be weary; and they shall walk, and not faint."**

NOT AGAINST FLESH AND BLOOD

Not fighting against flesh and blood means that your targets in the spiritual warfare are not human beings or living creatures with flesh and blood. Your targets are the devil and his demons.

Ephesians 6:12 lists the demonic armies and their hierarchies and formations by which the devil attacks human beings. They are fallen angels who rebelled against God's authority and were banished to the earth.

Principalities - These are the evil rulers or forces in the unseen world that oversee defined territories.

Powers – These are authorities and powerful satanic beings.

Rulers of the darkness of this world – These are the lords of the kingdom of darkness. They are highly placed evil spirits of darkness who rule this world, making use of the lower hierarchies of the "Powers" and "Principalities".

Spiritual wickedness in high places – These are spiritual powers of wickedness in the heavenly places; the huge numbers of wicked spirits in the unseen world. You can describe this literally as the headquarters of the wicked beings in the heavenly places.

THE WHOLE ARMOR OF GOD

You must put on the *whole armor of God* to be able to stand against all the wiles of the devil.

> When you pray to God, confess His words and believe Him for victory, don't add any other thing that God would not approve of. It is either God or nothing!

You are meant to *stand* firm and use these weapons. *Standing* connotes readiness; being alert spiritually, mentally, and physically. The platform on which you must stand should be Christ Jesus, the solid rock because every other ground is sinking sand. It's difficult if not impossible to wrestle and win when you're on the floor while your enemy is standing.

Let's briefly discuss these weapons of warfare.

TRUTH (BELT OF TRUTH)

You must have your loins tightened with truth, that is, the belt of truth.

Truth is a weapon. First, Jesus is the Way, the Truth, and the Life (Jn 14:6). And everything about Jesus – name, word, blood, and revelation – can be used as a weapon against the devil and his kingdom.

Every soldier's uniform includes a belt tied around their waists to make them look smart, spick and span. A soldier whose uniform is flabby risks entanglements with trees, grass, sticks and any form of obstacles around and may end up as a victim of war.

So, speaking truth or living a life of truth devoid of hypocrisy is a weapon against the spirit of falsehood or any form of waywardness that can get you stuck in ungodliness, deception, and illegalities.

BREASTPLATE OF RIGHTEOUSNESS

A breastplate is part of a soldier's uniform. It is a bulletproof vest that protects the heart against bullets and arrows. The heart is a vital body organ that no one can live without.

Righteousness is a right standing with God. Jesus was able to complete his earthly mission because of his right standing with God, having loved righteousness, and hated inequity (See Hebrews 1:8-10).

A breastplate of righteousness is important because you must protect your heart with righteousness against all manners of evils arrows launched to *steal* your heart (See John 10:10). Proverbs 4:23 says, "Guard your heart above all else, for it is the source of life." (HCSB). A good way to guard your heart is by being careful of what you store in and bring out from there.

FEET SHOD WITH PREPARATION OF GOSPEL OF PEACE

A foot connotes walking or a way of life.

The gospel of peace of Christ is that of peace, reconciliation, and freedom– from sins and evils that come with it.

So, arming your feet with gospel of peace connotes walking under the precepts of the gospel of Jesus Christ that brought peace for us. When your way of life conforms with the gospel of Christ, you're protected from devil's attacks. Proverbs 16:7 says, "When a man's ways please the LORD, he maketh even his enemies to be at peace with him."

SHIELD OF FAITH

A shield is a soldier's protective equipment from external aggressions. It's usually fastened to their faces to stop the penetrations of arrows and bullets.

A shield of faith is a defensive weapon to extinguish the fiery darts (flaming arrows) of the evil ones. Remember that we discussed a lot on how faith can get you unstuck under the law of faith in chapter seven. When your faith is rooted in God and his words of promise, his Holy Spirit would raise a standard against the arrows of the devil set against you.

Your face is another part of your body that must be jealously guarded. Remember, one stone hit Goliath's eye and he was on the floor. So, it's very important to exercise your faith in God such that when life's storms besiege you, you're unperturbed.

HELMET OF SALVATION

A soldier's helmet protects his head against external attacks (arrows of the enemy). Your head tells almost everything about you– your identity, brain works, eyes, mouths, etcetera. No one lives without a head! That's why it's very important to protect it.

While there are many available covers to "protect your head" during life's upheavals, salvation in Christ Jesus is the most secured. Acts 4:12 says, "And there is salvation in no one else; for there is no other name under heaven that has been given among people by which we must be saved [for God has provided the world no alternative for salvation]." (AMP) (See further Philippians 2:9-11, KJV; Psalm 91:14-16, GNT).

This salvation (that comes from repentance from sins) protects beyond earthly life experiences in that, even when death comes, you will continue to live in eternity with Christ Jesus. Therefore, live in the right standing with God, "work out your salvation [that is, cultivate it, bring it to full effect, actively pursue spiritual maturity] with awe-inspired fear and trembling [using serious caution and critical self-evaluation to avoid anything that might offend God or discredit the name of Christ]." (Phil 2:12, AMP).

SWORD OF THE SPIRIT

The sword of the Spirit is the word of God.

The sword of the Spirit appears to be the only offensive weapon in the list. Every other weapon appears defensive. God's word is multi-active and is not limited by distance or age – it never dies! Hebrews 4:12 says, "For the word of God is alive and powerful. It is sharper than the sharpest two-edged sword, cutting between soul and spirit, between joint and marrow. It exposes our innermost thoughts and desires." (NLT).

God is the Word, and the Word is God; the Word manifested in the flesh as Christ Jesus. (See Genesis 1:1; John 1:1). God's Word is his power unto salvation for all men. In other words, there's no other means by which God can save you outside of his Word.

The Centurion knew the impact of God's word and told Jesus, "… but speak the word only, and my servant shall be healed." (Matt 8:8). And that's what happened because God can't deny His word. His Word is efficacious because, "He sent his word, and healed them, and delivered them from their destructions." (Ps 107:20).

You must learn how to use the sword of the Spirit (word of God) adequately lest the devil twists it against your interest.

It was Eve's inadequate knowledge of God's instructions. (words) that made the serpent (Satan) hoodwink her into disobeying God's instructions (See Genesis chapters 2 & 3). The consequence of this singular disobedience has got humanity stuck to date!

Since your success and victory depend on God's word, you must learn, study, obey and live by it. You must also train and pray with it. As Apostle Paul instructed Timothy, "Study *and* do your best to present yourself to God approved, a workman [tested by trial] who has no reason to be ashamed, accurately handling *and* skillfully teaching the word of truth." (AMP).

A sword is a unique weapon but can only destroy what it's meant to destroy. It cannot destroy an armored tank, and neither can destroy ballistic missiles.

In the same way, it's not every *logos* on the pages of the holy Bible or every revelation (*rhema*) that is one-size-fit-all weapon. It's the target word that's meant for each attack that gives victory.

Lack of proper understanding of how to fight with the sword of the Spirit has wearied many believers and made them victims or left them in a backslidden state. They didn't get desired results even though they knew and used many scriptures.

When tempted by the devil, Jesus responded using the appropriate sword; *"It is written…"* When he was asked to turn stone to bread, he didn't quote the text about God's protection but the ones that related to the temptation: "It is written, Man shall not live by bread alone…" (Matt 4:4). This is using the appropriate sword to fight a particular battle. This is how to fight with the sword of the Spirit and win.

PRAYING ALWAYS

Since all these weapons are spiritual, you've got to launch them invisibly.

A potent way of achieving this is the instrumentality of unceasing prayers– supplication (earnest petition). This must be Spirit-directed and not just mere babbling. Jesus was earnest in prayers. (See Hebrews 5:7; Luke 22:44). Apostle Paul was also a good example (See II Corinthians 12:8).

It is important to persevere because God is not your stooge or an errand boy to be sent to supply your order at any given time. He will answer your prayers at the nick of time – a time that he alone knows is the best for you. See Ecclesiastes Chapter 3.

The beauty of the efficacious prayers of the saints lies in the fact that it not only works for you alone but also gets others unstuck once it's offered in line with God's will. That's why Paul personally requested it for "all saints" including himself (Eph 6:18-19).

It is noteworthy that Paul wrote the book of Ephesians which outlines these unique warfare principles while in prison. He was being persecuted for preaching the gospel of Christ Jesus. He knew that when prayers are launched, the beneficiaries must get unstuck. He asked for prayers from the Ephesian church such that "utterance may be given … to make known the mystery of the gospel" for which he was an "ambassador in bonds…" (Ephesians 6:19-20, KJV).

PLATFORMS OF OPERATION

Before we end this chapter, let's briefly talk about related subjects of spiritual warfare.

Recall that we talked earlier in this chapter about the principalities, powers, rulers of the darkness of this world and the spiritual wickedness in high places. These are the demonic formations through which the devil steals, kills and destroys people's joy and lives.

These demonic ranks operate in platforms which are not limited to the heavenly realms or geographic environments but extend to your soul realm– your mind, imaginations, and thoughts. All of these are demonic strongholds with which you engage your spiritual weapons which "… are mighty through God to the pulling down of strong holds." (II Cor 10:4).

In chapter one, I stated that we're not in the valley of Elah anymore. *Our valley of Elah is now everywhere, including our minds.*

With your weapons, you cast down "imaginations" and "every high thing" that exalts itself against the knowledge of God. These are false arguments about God's word regarding your situation and the devil's fine-sounding arguments contradicting God's word.

Satan argued God's word with Eve in Genesis chapter 3, asking, *"Has God really said...", "you shall not surely die...".*

Another example was when Satan tempted Jesus in Matthew chapter 4. Can you imagine the devil telling Jesus, *"If you are the son of God..."* and promising to give him the kingdoms of the earth and their splendor?

Is the devil telling you to commit suicide? Or that you would soon die? Or that you would never come out of debts or that you would be barren? These are his arguments against God's will for you. Don't panic. He did the same to Jesus Christ.

Devil's first platform for attack is your mind. But like Jesus, pull such "imaginations" down, "bringing into captivity every thought to the obedience of Christ..." You must be quick to use God' word as "it is written" and declare it without fear. You must also guard your mind and your heart with God's word knowing that they are the wellsprings of life.

In order to bring demons into obedience, your obedience to God's word must be complete. It's by your obedience that you "revenge all disobedience" of the devil. *If you don't care about God's instructions, then the devil won't care about what you say, even if you call Jesus' name a million times!*

When you closely examine the spiritual weapons discussed under Ephesians 6, you'll discover that there's no recommended covering for your back. This is not an omission. God's got your back once you're not lazy with the weapons committed to you. God has promised to uphold you with His righteous right hand and to be with you till the end of the age. (See Isaiah 41:10; Matthew 28:20).

Even when you appear stuck after all has been done, God's got your back and would not hold your victory back. The devil's principality (the prince of Persia) resisted Daniel's answered prayers for twenty-one days. Daniel was not unstuck until Angel Michael (who was superior to the principality of Persia) came to his rescue. (See Daniel 10:12-13).

When earthly wisdom and principles are applied and you still stay stuck, engage the spiritual weapons. At the nick of time, God will come through for you. Amen!

EPILOGUE

"And when Saul saw David go forth against the Philistine, he said unto Abner, the captain of the host, Abner, whose son is this youth? And Abner said, As thy soul liveth, O king, I cannot tell. And the king said, Enquire thou whose son the stripling is. And as David returned from the slaughter of the Philistine, Abner took him, and brought him before Saul with the head of the Philistine in his hand. And Saul said to him, Whose son art thou, thou young man? And David answered, I am the son of thy servant Jesse the Bethlehemite."

- I Samuel 17:55-58

Did you notice something strange in I Samuel 17:55-58?

David had killed Goliath when King Saul asked his chief commander, Abner, whose son David was. Worst, the Army Commander was ignorant of who David was.

Wait a minute. What's going on here?

What if David was a traitor? Why didn't they run a five-minute search on David or continue to carry out background check on him as battle raged? Earlier in verses 37 and 38, King Saul had conversations with David and even offered to help with his armor. Wasn't this a good time to get to know David better? Was the battle so urgent that no one considered vetting David before or during the battle? Perhaps!

God bypassed protocols and raised David to meet the exigencies of the moment. Getting unstuck sometimes requires God to break protocols in order to get you to a fulfilment. And when God breaks man's protocols, He ensures that nothing goes wrong!

Your problems might have been given some labels that are intimidating, such that each time you think about those titles or labels, it breaks your heart. You are familiar with expressions such as

"That sickness has killed sizeable numbers of people", "That much dreaded pandemic has no cure", "Only 1 out of 10 patients survives that disease", the list goes on!

Goliath was labeled "giant", "champion", and a soldier who had "... been fighting from his youth", all of which wrenched the Israelites' hearts. Even when Goliath was not talking, his followers' chants and songs of approval were strident. After all, their champion never conceded defeats to anyone, and the gods of the Philistines had their back.

But Goliath's labels endured until a game-changer arose and his titles faded when David appeared. The Philistines' accolades were silenced, and the echoers of premature victories soon disappeared into the thin air. Goliath's head was severed from his neck and his hitherto titles became useless.

David changed the game and the timid Israelites jubilated in ecstasy.

The sundry titles of your problems will no longer endure when God arises in your favor and breaks protocols and barriers to your freedom.

Allowing David to lead a fight against Israelites' greatest enemy without vetting him is a demonstration of a breach of protocols. But because it was God's doing, nothing went bad.

People who were condemned to death had found pardon at the last minute. Women who should have died during labor had given birth and now alive. Heinous edicts meant to destroy many people's lives had been abrogated in the past. Patients who had had "Do Not Resuscitate" on their bodies have come back to life and remained alive.

Children who had suffered great "disability" have grown to become "bests" in their respective fields. There have been the worst of criminals who became well-behaved individuals and preachers of

God's word. Yes, it does happen that the stone rejected by the builders have become capstone (See Psalms 118:22), especially when God breaks protocols to get his people unstuck.

Let God arise and bless your efforts. When he is charge, nothing goes wrong. Hold on to God in faith, sing his testimonies, hope in him, and he will get you unstuck. Amen!

DAVID AND CHRIST JESUS SHARE COMMON TRAITS

David worked. He was excellent in skills, diligent in tasks, dignified in labor, and victorious in battles. He practiced all his known principles - faith, prayers, consultation, positive confession, positive perspective, and sang songs of testimonies. He did not stop there. He swung into action; he was up and doing. His God-inspired actions killed Goliath.

David willingly assumed responsibility, stepped into the arena of the battle, dared the consequences, and killed the giant from whom many mighty soldiers retreated. There, at the valley of Elah, the Israelites were freed from the powerful giant.

David's descendant, Jesus Christ, also willingly assumed responsibility, stooped low to the status of humanity, came to the earth, and nailed the *giant called sin* to the cross– this giant that's been terrorizing humanity since the fall of Adam and Eve.

Before he was unstuck, a blind man begging for alms at the roadside asked what was going on when Jesus was nearby. The crowd told him, "Jesus of Nazareth" was passing-by. The blind man beckoned to him and shouted, "Jesus, Son of David, have mercy on me!" Even when rebuked and told to be quiet, he shouted more stridently, "Jesus, Son of David, have mercy on me!"

The blind man appealed to Jesus through his descent and not his geographical birthplace. This caught Jesus' attention. Of course, Jesus healed him immediately. (See Luke 18:35-43).

In your quest to get unstuck, *see beyond the crowd and stretch beyond your limitations*. Raise your voice louder than that of naysayers who're shouting you down. Appeal to Jesus' mercy and invoke His covenant heritage name.

The winning Spirit will help you to get unstuck.

Amen!

In Honor of David Jesse, The Slayer of Goliath

Giving meaning to life and unto the Truth appeal to get
unstuck
Not unto self alone live until future a cinch
David, when life's vicissitudes lurk and weapons suck
In faith, confessing with might then act the *giant* to lynch

In altitude of attitude always flying
Not fearing nor betraying in face of sword darted
With no lens of sense denying
Contemplating, collective, yet in process rooted, wisdom
crafted

Neither in loss nor in defeat but in victory songs of melody he
sings
Rising above accolades, *giant's* hacks and violence subdued
In covenant hid with identity as His name wins
Till rock of covenant *giant's* eye blinded

Therefore, live now your life, and for a cause stay
Purpose bigger, destiny larger than your size
At the end, "a man came and difference made", they'll say,
"The world a better place because he came to pay the price."

Kudos to Jesse's youngest son
of uncommon bravado
Bravo, David!

'Segun Adepoju
June 2021.

ENDNOTES

Chapter 1

1. Steve Brachmann, "The Evolution of Wind Shield Wipers – A Patent History", https://www.ipwatchdog.com/2014/11/09/the-evolution-of-wind-shield-wipers-a-patent-history/id=52085/

2. Songsfacts, https://www.songfacts.com/facts/don-moen/god-will-make-a-way
3. Nick Glass and Tim Hume, CNN, The 'hallelujah moment' behind the invention of the Post-it note, https://www.cnn.com/2013/04/04/tech/post-it-note-history/index.html
4. Robert H. Schuller, Turning Your Hurts into Halos, Thomas Nelson (May, 2000).

Chapter 2

1. Stan Toler, The Power of Your Attitude (Harvest House Publisher, 2016), 15
2. Quoted in "The Good and the Bad in Each Day", in "A Pastor's Heart" January 22, 2013 Edition, https://apastorsheart.com/tag/rick-warren/

3. The Seattle Times, "people In Sports", Oct 7, 1996, https://archive.seattletimes.com/archive/?date=19971007&slug=2564710
4. Phil Luza, How Sir. Edmund Hillary Conquered Mt. Everest, https://medium.com/adventure-capitalists/4-legendary-ways-to-make-your-own-luck-12ed3e9e9e38
5. Credited to Polonius in Shakespeare's "Hamlet".

Chpater 3

1. Dr. Don Colbert, *What You Don't Know May be Killing You* (Siloam, A Strang Company), 2.
2. Op Cit, 4

Chapter 4

1. Lysa Terkeurst, *Forgiving What You Can't Forget,* (Nashville: Thomas Nelson, 2020), 29.
2. Lysa Terkeurst, *Op. Cit, 47*
3. Tyler Perry's Emotional Story: Why I Forgave My Abusive Father/People TV/Entertainment weekly, Oct. 23, 2017, https://www.youtube.com/watch?v=UB-9znO4dF0s

Chapter 5

1. Dan Morain, *Kamala's Way,* (Simon & Schuster, 2021), 172.
2. MindTools, "Lewin's Change Management, https://www.mindtools.com/pages/article/newPPM_94.htm
3. Walter Dean Meyers, *A Biography of Malcom X, By Any Means Necessary* (Scholastic

Focus, 2020), 35.

4. Les Brown, "IT IS NOT OVER UNTIL YOU WIN", Georgia Dome, (Les Brown's Greatest Hits), https://www.youtube.com/watch?v=8Fd06U-3TAY&feature=youtu.be

5. Philip Paul Bliss (1838-1876) "I Am So Glad That Jesus Loves Me", https://www.wholesomewords.org/biography/biobliss8.html

Chapter 6
1. Christy Ogbeide, *In Search of a Child,* (El-Shaddai Publishers, 2000), 70.
2. Christy Ogbeide, OP Cit., 71.

Chapter 7
1. David McCasland, *The Quotable of Oswald Chambers*, (Oswald Chambers Publications Association, Ltd, 2008) 94.

Chapter 8
1. Stephen R. Covey, *The 7 Habits of Highly Effective People,* (Free Press, 1989, 2004), 262-263.

2. The United States of America's Office of the Historian, "*U.S.-Soviet Alliance, 1941–1945*", https://history.state.gov/milestones/1937-1945/us-soviet

3. Carter Smith, Presidents, Haylas Publishing, 2004, at P. 192

Chapter 9
1. Kathie Lee Gifford, *It's Never Too Late,* (W Publishing Group, 2020), 51.
2. Kathie Lee Gifford's Biography, http://www.kathieleegifford.com/biography/
3. Kathie Lee Gifford, *It's Never Too Late,* (W Publishing Group, 2020), 15.
4. Kathie Lee Gifford, *OP Cit., 16*
5. Chain Mail, https://en.wikipedia.org/wiki/Chain_mail
6. "Perfection" as used in this sense is not being used in the context of Matthew 5:48 which says we should be perfect for our heavenly father is perfect. In Genesis 17:1, God told Abram to walk before Him and be perfect. So, when you do what God says you should do, you're perfect in that action. But as used in the sentence, it means, "Except it's God who's specifically instructing you to do a thing, don't expect a perfect condition of things before acting; don't expect to act when you think you're faultless to make mistakes."

Chapter 10
1. https://en.wikipedia.org/wiki/List_of_organs_of_the_human_body
2. https://www.healthline.com/health/number-of-cells-in-body#types-of-cells
3. https://en.wikipedia.org/wiki/Milky_Way
4. https://en.wikipedia.org/wiki/Terrestrial_planet
5. https://www.space.com/16080-solar-system-planets.html
6. Demosthenes, https://en.wikipedia.org/wiki/Demosthenes

7. Zig Ziglar, Top Performance, (Fleming H. Revell, 1986) P.11.

8. **Emma Berthold**, "AI and the robotics revolution", https://www.science.org.au/ curious/technology-future/ai-and-robotics-revolution.

9. Emma Berthold, Op Cit.

10. https://en.wikipedia.org/wiki/Cognitive_skill.

11. Kai Zhou [1], ED/GEMR/MRT/2016/P1/5, Non-cognitive skills: definitions, measurement and malleability, p.2, published in "https://unesdoc.unesco.org/ ark:/48223/pf0000245576#:~:text=Non%2Dcognitive%20skills%20are%20 defined,personal%20traits%2C%20attitudes%20and%20motivations."

Chapter 11

1. https://www2.cs.uic.edu/~jbell/CourseNotes/OperatingSystems/blindMen.html

2. Stephen R. Covey et al, *First Things First*, (Simons & Schuster UK Ltd, 1994) P. 27

3. Stephen R. Covey, *The 7 Habits of Highly effective People*, (FP Free Press) 1989, 2004, @28-29

4. https://www.happinessacademy.eu/blog-en/a-tale-of-the-pear-and-its-four-seasons

5. Lysa terkeurst, *Forgiving What You Can't Forget*, (Nashville: Thomas Nelson, 2020) 74.

6. Lysa terkeurst, *page 80*

7. Lysa terkeurst, *pages 82-83*.

Chapter 14

1. A Psalm of Life, By Henry Wadsworth Longfellow, https://www.poetryfoundation.org/poems/44644/a-psalm-of-life

2. Leo Buscaglia, "Risks", Quotable Quotes: https://www.goodreads.com/ quotes/6531047-risks-to-laugh-is-to-risk-appearing-a-fool-to

3. The Wright Brothers' National memorial https://www.nps.gov/wrbr/learn/historyculture/thefirstflight.htm